Cambridge Elements ≡

Elements in Development Economics
Series Editor-in-Chief
Kunal Sen
UNU-WIDER and University of Manchester

PARENTAL INVESTMENTS AND CHILDREN'S HUMAN CAPITAL IN LOW-TO-MIDDLE-INCOME COUNTRIES

Jere R. Behrman
University of Pennsylvania

T0349755

UNITED NATIONS
UNIVERSITY
UNU-WIDER

CAMBRIDGE
UNIVERSITY PRESS

CAMBRIDGE
UNIVERSITY PRESS

Shaftesbury Road, Cambridge CB2 8EA, United Kingdom

One Liberty Plaza, 20th Floor, New York, NY 10006, USA

477 Williamstown Road, Port Melbourne, VIC 3207, Australia

314–321, 3rd Floor, Plot 3, Splendor Forum, Jasola District Centre,
New Delhi – 110025, India

103 Penang Road, #05–06/07, Visioncrest Commercial, Singapore 238467

Cambridge University Press is part of Cambridge University Press & Assessment,
a department of the University of Cambridge.

We share the University's mission to contribute to society through the pursuit of
education, learning and research at the highest international levels of excellence.

www.cambridge.org
Information on this title: www.cambridge.org/9781009336161

DOI: 10.1017/9781009336147

First published 2022

A catalogue record for this publication is available from the British Library.

ISBN 978-1-009-33616-1 Paperback
ISSN 2755-1601 (online)
ISSN 2755-1598 (print)

Parental Investments and Children's Human Capital in Low-to-Middle-Income Countries

Elements in Development Economics

DOI: 10.1017/9781009336147
First published online: November 2022

Jere R. Behrman
University of Pennsylvania
Author for correspondence: Jere R. Behrman, jbehrman@econ.upenn.edu

Abstract: This Element reviews what we know about parental investments and children's human capital in low-to-middle-income countries (LMICs). First, it presents definitions and a simple analytical framework; then discusses determinants of children's human capital in the form of cognitive skills, socioemotional skills and physical and mental health; then reviews estimates of impacts of these forms of human capital; next considers the implications of such estimates for inequality and poverty; and concludes with a summary suggesting some positive impacts of parental investments on children's human capital in LMICs and a discussion of gaps in the literature pertaining to both data and methodology. This title is also available as Open Access on Cambridge Core.

Keywords: human capital, parental investments, cognitive skills, socioemotional skills, health

ISBNs: 9781009336161 (PB), 9781009336147 (OC)
ISSNs: 2755-1601 (online), 2755-1598 (print)

Contents

1 Introduction

Human capital in various forms – cognitive skills, socioemotional skills and physical and mental health –is widely considered critical for many dimensions of individual fulfillment and for successful development in low- and middle-income countries (LMICs). Indeed, the extent and distribution of human capital is thought by many to be at the heart of the development process. Many proximal determinants of most children's human capital are in their parental families and the investments that parents make in their children. The relation between parental and children's characteristics, including human capital, is also closely tied to inequality in the children's generation and to social mobility – the potential to move from a lower to a higher level of education, occupational status, social class, or income. Greater equality and greater social mobility for many are major hopes of economic development and the mantra of a good society. Social mobility may be intergenerational (children's outcomes in comparison with their parents') or intragenerational (within children's lifecycles), and social mobility may be absolute (are children better off than their parents?) or relative (in comparison with other members of the same generation, in which case upward mobility for one individual must be accompanied by downward mobility for at least one other individual) (Deutscher and Mazumder, 2021; Behrman, 2022; Iversen et al., 2022). Concerns about rising inequality have engendered renewed Interest not only in how human capital relates to inequality but also in social mobility, including in LMICs as well as in high-income countries (HICs).

This book assesses what we know – and do not know – about the role of parental investments in children's human capital and how those investments relate to inequality and poverty in the children's generation and to social mobility in LMICs, as well as how market imperfections such as information and credit constraints faced by low-income households may impede parental investments in their children's human capital and thereby social mobility. The focus is on parental investments in children's human capital, but these relations are clearly related to the nature of distribution in the children's generation and to social mobility, so some limited attention is also paid to distribution and social mobility.

Section 2 presents definitions for human capital and parental endowments, simple frameworks for guiding the summary of what we know and do not know about the roles of parental human capital and parental endowments in children's human capital in LMICs and what are the estimation challenges in learning about these relations. Section 3 discusses the determinants of children's human capital in the form of cognitive skills, socioemotional skills, and physical and mental health. Section 4 turns to the impacts of these forms of human capital on indicators of welfare such as incomes and earnings and thereby on inequality and poverty. Section 5 considers the implications of estimates such as summarized in the previous two sections for inequality and poverty in the children's generation. Section 6 concludes with a summary of the material covered in this book and a discussion of gaps in the literature related to data, methodology, and topics.[1]

2 Definitions, Framework, and Estimation Issues

Definitions

Human capital is a vector of stock outcomes at any point in the lifecycle that reflects the accumulation of net investments in humans up to that point in their lifecycles that have longer-run returns/impacts over the rest of their lifecycles in terms of income, occupation, and other outcomes. Human capital is multidimensional: cognitive skills, socioemotional skills, physical, and mental wellbeing. Human capital is <u>not</u> the same as schooling attainment, though some literature implicitly or explicitly equates the two. Schooling attainment may be one important input/investment into the production of important forms of human capital, in particular cognitive development. But even for cognitive skills, schooling attainment is not likely the only important input. There are likely to be other important inputs, such as early-life nutrition and stimulation, the nature of the home environment throughout childhood and adolescence, and the characteristics ("qualities") of schools. Moreover, in LMIC contexts, other forms of human capital may be critical, including physical and mental health and nutritional status. Recent estimates in *The Lancet*, for example, are that ~250 million children under 5 years of age in LMICs are at risk of not reaching their developmental potential (Lu et al., 2016; Black et al., 2017). The primary indicator used for these estimates, accounting for ~170 million children, is chronic undernourishment as reflected in stunting (defined as length/height less than two standard deviations below the medians for well-nourished populations).

---

[1] A note about the sources used for this book is useful. There are huge literatures on some of the topics that are covered, for example, entire handbooks on one form of human capital, education. Relatedly, as background for this book, a systematic search was undertaken on one topic related to the coverage of this book, human capital and mobility in LMICs and 132 studies were identified in the last three years alone, and they do not include all of the relevant studies. It is not possible to review all the related literature in a study of this size, so of necessity the coverage is selective based in part on what studies arguably provide causal evidence on the impact of parental investments on children's human capital and the impacts of children's human capital on other outcomes of interest.

Parental endowments are also a vector including elements such as economic resources, health, marital status, education, genetic factors, and social connections, not all of which are observed in most (any?) data sets.

Framework

Figure 1 gives a very simple framework of optimal investments in and resulting human capital stocks of children over their lifecycles with five lifecycle stages: (1) Early Life, (2) Preschool Ages, (3) Childhood and Adolescence, (4) Young Adulthood, and 5) Mature Adulthood. The designation of these particular lifecycle stages is somewhat arbitrary, but captures fairly well essential elements of the current literatures that are discussed below, including the possibilities of critical windows of opportunities particularly in early life. These stages focus on the "children's" generation to contrast with the previous parental or familial generation. For each lifecycle stage children start with the accumulated human capital vector from the previous stage, which influences the rate of return to investments in the current stage through dynamic complementarities across stages, with possibilities of critical windows of opportunities usually emphasized most for the early stages and in some cases for adolescence (Cunha et al., 2006; Cunha and Heckman, 2008; Cunha et al., 2010; Black et al., 2021). There are also static complementarities among different components of children's human capital within stages, so that, e.g., better nutrition may improve concurrent learning. Within each stage there are

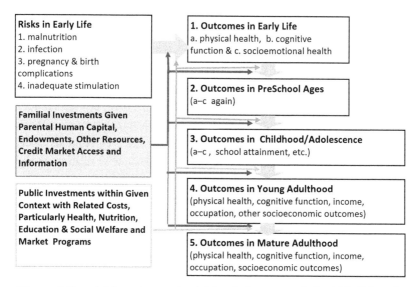

Figure 1 Parental investments in children's human capital within lifecycle framework

also family inputs/investments (shaded box on left) and public investments (box on lower left), among the elements of which there also may be complementarities. These investments occur within a lifecycle framework with demand-side (parental family) and supply-side (health clinics, preschools, schools, training programs, credit markets, information markets) determinants, the returns to which depend on policy environments and markets over the lifecycle. Parental human capital and endowments may affect children's development over the children's lifecycles. Even though the direct effects of parental human capital and endowments are likely to be focused in the earlier lifecycle stages, the indirect effects are likely to percolate from the earlier to the later stages though the accumulated child human capital from stage to stage (Black et al., 2021; Black et al., Forthcoming). Similarly, policies may have direct effects on any particular lifecycle stage and indirect effects on subsequent stages. Thus human capital of the parents and their endowments play major roles as determinants of developments over the lifecycles of their children, and human capital of the children play major roles as an outcome of interest in itself and of transferring effects across lifecycle stages. The motives for parental investments in their children's human capital may in part be altruism (which may be inversely associated with parental socioeconomic status (Das, 2007)), but they may also be to increase the probabilities of reverse transfers when the parents become elderly. The latter motive is likely to be more important in LMICs than in HICs because of less-developed social security and old-age pension systems (Lillard and Willis, 1997).

Parental investments in children's human capital are likely to be associated with the distribution of income and other outcomes in the children's generation, including social mobility. Intergenerational social mobility typically refers to how correlated are elements of parental characteristics (e.g., schooling, occupation, income) with the same elements of children's characteristics preferably, but not always, at the same lifecycle stage or, better yet, age within lifecycle stages (Deutscher and Mazumder, 2021; Iversen et al., 2022). Intragenerational mobility refers to how correlated are children's characteristics across different stages (or ages) of the children's lifecycle. The less such correlations ceteris paribus, the greater is said to be mobility, whether absolute or relative (though for relative mobility the ceteris paribus may include the absolute mobility of all other children).

Economic models of what determine parental investments in their children focus on perceived marginal costs and marginal returns to such investments given parental human capital and endowments and market and policy contexts. At one extreme with perfect markets including those for information and for capital, the equilibrium human capital of the child is determined as in the Becker Woytinsky Lecture (Becker, 1967) (Figure 2a) and the Becker and

Tomes "wealth model" (Becker and Tomes, 1976; Becker and Tomes, 1986; Becker, 1991; Behrman et al., 1995). With all markets perfect, this equilibrium human capital stock H_0 is where the expected rate of return (the solid downward-sloping line – downward-sloping because of diminishing returns due to fixed child endowments such as innate abilities and health) on human capital equals the market rate of interest for credit (the horizontal solid line, indicating that the marginal cost to the family does not change in this case with the investment level given perfect capital markets). Note that in this case, two children who are identical including in their endowments but from very different families in terms of parental human capital and parental endowments have the same equilibrium human capital stocks. But the assumption of perfect markets is extremely strong and requires not only perfect capital and information markets but also perfect markets for other inputs such as parental endowments including genetic endowments and all the inputs into early life nurturing care (Black et al., 2017; Britto et al., 2017; Richter et al., 2017; Black et al., 2021). Given that there are not markets for parental genetic endowments and there is considerable evidence that genetic endowments are intergenerationally correlated, for example, even if all other markets were perfect, children with higher parental genetic endowments all else equal on average would have higher expected rates of return to every human capital level if, as is widely believed, genetic ability endowments are complementary with human capital, such as in the dashed line in Figure 2a – and thus a higher level of equilibrium human capital H_a.

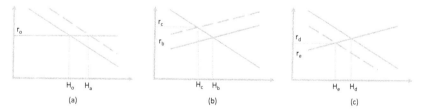

Figure 2 Becker's Woytinsky Lecture: Intersection of marginal rate of return and marginal costs determine equilibrium interest rate (r) and equilibrium human capital (H). (**a**) Downward-sloping marginal rate of return and constant marginal costs, with dashed line giving higher marginal rate of return for each H. (**b**) Downward-sloping marginal rate of return and upward-sloping marginal costs, with dashed line giving higher marginal costs for each H. (**c**) Downward-sloping marginal rate of return and upward-sloping marginal costs, with dashed line giving lower marginal rate or return for each H

Source: Author's drawings.

If capital markets are not perfect, all else equal, the marginal costs of capital are likely to be upward-sloping for any given child/family as in Figure 2b, with cheaper access for families with more resources (solid line) in comparison with households with less resources (dashed line), resulting in higher child human capital in the former (H_b) than the latter (H_c) ceteris paribus. Also, if capital markets are not perfect, parents may maximize their utilities by investing less in some or all of their children than would be required to equate the expected marginal rates of return on their children's human capital to equal the marginal costs of human capital (Behrman et al., 1995). For such reasons parental resources are likely to determine child human capital if capital markets are not perfect. If the only imperfection is in information markets and better-informed households have higher expected returns to every level of human capital as in the solid line in Figure 2c than less-well-informed households (dashed line in Figure 2c), the equilibrium human capital is higher for the better-informed households (H_d) than for the less-well-informed households (H_e). The general perception, reinforced by some empirical studies (Jensen, 2010; Dizon-Ross, 2019), is that parental families with more resources have higher expectations about the returns to human capital than do poorer households.

Further, note that parents may have other objectives than simply maximizing the expected wealth of the next generation. For example, the Separable-Earnings-Transfers (SET) model posits that parents also care about the distribution of potential earnings among their children when they invest in their children's human capital (Behrman et al., 1982b). Figure 3a illustrates parental preferences defined over human-capital-dependent earnings of two children if the parents have no concern about distribution among their children (straight line), extreme Rawlsian concern about distribution among their children (L-shaped or Leontieff), or an intermediate case with productivity-equity trade-offs (curved line). Figure 3b shows the determination of the equilibrium human capital of the two children for an intermediate case of parental preferences regarding inequality among their children's human-capital-dependent expected earnings with a earnings-possibility production function (solid line) elongated in the direction of child 2 to reflect that child 2 has greater innate earnings endowments than child 1 or the expected labor market rates of return for equal human capital are greater for child 2 than for child 1 (e.g., labor-market discrimination that favors males and child 2 is male and child 1 is female) (Rosenzweig and Schultz, 1982). If the parents have equal concern so that the preference curves are symmetrical around the 45° ray from the origin, the equilibrium human capital is greater in child 2 than in child 1 ($H_2 > H_1$) except in the extreme case of Rawlsian preferences, but parental investments compensate at least some for endowment differences among their children except in the

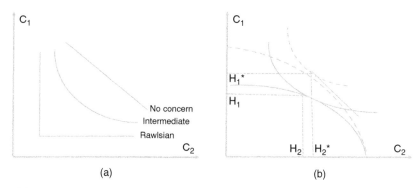

Figure 3 Parental preferences and allocation of human capital between two children. (**a**) Parental preferences regarding earnings distribution between Child 1 (C_1) and Child 2 (C_2): No concern about distribution (linear), intermediate (curved), and extreme (L-shaped). (**b**) Earnings production possibility frontier favoring Child 2 (C_2) (solid line) shifted somewhat to disfavor Child 1 (C_1) less so that equilibrium moves from (H_1, H_2) to (H_1^*, H_2^*)

Source: Author's drawing.

extreme case of linear preferences. If parents have unequal concern (e.g., favoring boys or lower-order births), the preference curves are not symmetrical around the 45° ray but shifted in the direction of the types favored by parents, which results in higher human capital for the favored child all else equal. Empirical estimates of this model suggest that parental preferences are significantly different from what would be required for simple wealth maximization for the next generation, with considerable concern about distribution among children in families in a range of societies including Chile, India, and the United States and with unequal concern tending to favor sons and lower birth orders (Behrman et al., 1982a; Behrman et al., 1986; Behrman and Taubman, 1986; Taubman and Behrman, 1986; Behrman, 1988b; Behrman, 1988a; Abufhele et al., 2017). If parents are concerned about the expected distribution of human-capital-dependent earnings among their children, in general they will not invest in all children so that the marginal rates of return on human capital are equal to the marginal costs for each child.

Finally, the parents may not have an unified preference function, in which case parental human capital embodied in and resources under the control of mothers are likely to have different (usually perceived to be stronger) effects than those for fathers or there may be stronger mother-daughter and father-son effects than cross-gender intergenerational effects (Rosenzweig and Schultz, 1982; Rosenzweig and Schultz, 1984; King and Lillard, 1987; Schultz, 1990; Thomas, 1990; Thomas et al., 1991; Thomas and Strauss,

1992; Thomas, 1993; Lillard and Willis, 1994; Alderman et al., 1995; Haddad et al., 1996). Thus a number of dimensions of household composition may be important in determining the effects of parental human capital and endowments on child human capital and other outcomes. Moreover the family may be embedded in a larger kin network, so that human capital and endowments of other kin (e.g., grandparents, uncles, aunts) or ethnic group members may affect investments in children, perhaps resulting, for example, in lower social mobility than would appear to be the case were parents alone considered (Jones, 1998; Zeng and Xie, 2014; Reynolds et al., 2018; Chakraborty et al., 2019).

This framework directly applies to parental investments in children and to the resulting distribution in the children's generation of income and other outcomes, as well as to absolute social mobility, whether inter- or intra-generational. Using the implied relations between parental characteristics and children's outcomes, for example, one can estimate the impact of changing parental characteristics on the distribution of income and other outcomes of interest, as well as the extent of absolute mobility in terms of, say, income or schooling attainment, between parents and their children or between different lifecycle stages for the children. For relative social mobility the question, of course, is how do movements (again, whether inter- or intra-generational) for a particular child compare with movements for other children.

One final important point is that the empirical use of this general framework will always be within particular historical market, policy, and sociocultural contexts. For one illustration, the expected-earnings-productivity frontier in Figure 3b depends not only on family and child characteristics, but, as noted, on market, political and cultural factors that may relate to demographic characteristics of the children such as ethnicity, race, and gender. If child 1 is a female and child 2 a male, for example and new policies are introduced or norms change in ways that favor females more than previously, the expected-earnings-productivity frontier would increase in the vertical dimension as in the dashed line and generally increase the equilibrium human capital of child 1 (H_1^*) relative to child 2 (H_2^*). The various dimensions of the context are likely to vary substantially between LMICs and HICs, as well as among and within LIMICs because of different degrees of market development inter alia. That means that it would be naïve to assume without further empirical testing that the impact of parental human capital and parental endowments on children's human capital and on social mobility from one context automatically carries over to other contexts. What happens in one context may be suggestive of what relations may be like in another context, but care need be taken with generalizations that are not tested in other contexts, the more so the more important are nonlinearities including interactions and the more different are the contexts.

Estimation Issues in Investigating Impacts of Parental Human Capital and Endowments on Children's Human Capital

In all applied econometrics the nature and the quality of the available data are critical. First, many variables that are observed are measured with considerable error, which if random tends to bias the coefficient estimates of such variables toward zero when they are used as right-side variables, a bias that is exacerbated with fixed-effects estimates (e.g., siblings or within-family estimates). Instrumental variables can be used to control for these random measurement errors (e.g., reports on schooling from other sources for sibling fixed-effects estimates under assumption that the errors in such reports are not correlated with the errors in own reports (Ashenfelter and Krueger, 1994; Behrman et al., 1994) as are used in some of the studies summarized below (Behrman et al., 2015; Hu et al., 2021).

Second, a number of important variables are not observed in the data used to investigate the relations between parental human capital and parental endowments and children's human capital in LMICs. Leading examples are information on mental health and on components of intergenerationally correlated endowments, such as genetics and family culture and family connections. For example, consider the following relations between human capital and endowments of parents and human capital of children that are an extension of the model in Behrman and Taubman (1985). Assume as in relation (1) that Z is an outcome for which intergenerational social mobility is being estimated (e.g., income, occupation, cognitive skills, schooling attainment for children (c)) that depends linearly on the same outcome for the children's parents (p), child endowments E, and a stochastic term u for random events and measurement error in Z_c:

$$Z_c = a_0 + a_p Z_p + a_e E_c + u_c \qquad (1)$$

The endowments are included in this relation (though not in most two- or multi-generational studies) because there are likely to be unobserved multigenerationally correlated genetic, environmental, and preference factors that are likely to affect Z_c, as emphasized in the discussion of Figure 1 above. Assume that these endowments are correlated across generations and generated by:

$$E_c = b_0 + b_p E_p + v_c \qquad (2)$$

To understand the implications of these endowments for the estimation of the causal parental effect a_p in relation (1), assume that the parameters in (1) are stable across generations and that a one-generation-lagged version of relation (1) in which gp refers to grandparents determines Z_p:

$$Z_p = a_0 + a_p Z_{gp} + a_e E_p + u_p \tag{1A}$$

The estimation problem due to unobserved multigenerationally correlated endowments is immediately obvious. The compound disturbance term in relation (1) is $a_e E_c + u_c$, which includes E_c – but E_c depends on E_p (relation 2) and Z_p also depends on E_p (relation 1A), so Z_p is correlated with the compound disturbance term. As a result, the ordinary-least-squares (OLS) estimate of the a_p is biased unless either a_e or $b_p = 0$ because in addition to the impact of Z_p the OLS estimate of a_p includes the correlated impact of the unobserved multigenerationally correlated endowments. One way to deal with this estimation problem is to use good instruments for Z_p. Another way is to manipulate relations (1), (2) and (1A) to eliminate the endowments and obtain:

$$Z_c = (a_0 + a_e b_0 - b_p a_0) + (a_p + b_p)Z_p - (b_p a_p)Z_{gp} + (v_c + u_c - b_p u_p)$$
$$= c_0 + c_1 Z_p + c_2 Z_{gp} + w_c \tag{3}$$

Several aspects of this relation merit note:

(1) It is of the same general form as the relations typically used to estimate what are widely interpreted to be grandparental effects such as in a version of relation (1) without endowments.

(2) The coefficients of the right-side parental variable Z_p are NOT the parental effects, but the sum of the true parental effects a_p and the multigenerational coefficient on endowments b_p. The estimated coefficients of the right-side parental variable Z_p, therefore, are upward-biased estimates of the true parental effects a_p if multigenerational endowments are positively correlated (in which case b_p is positive).

(3) The coefficients of the right-side grandparental vector Z_{gp} are NOT the grandparental effects, but depend on the true parental effects a_p and the multigenerational endowment-generating parameter b_p and do not capture direct grandparental effects.

(4) The coefficients on the right-side parental vector Z_p and the right-side grandparental vector Z_{gp} can be solved (or estimated directly with nonlinear estimators) to obtain estimates of the parental effects a_p and the multigenerational coefficient on endowments b_p that are not contaminated by biases due to unobserved multigenerationally correlated endowments that are generated by relation (2).

(5) OLS estimates of relation (3) nevertheless result in biased estimates of the coefficients of Z_p because the disturbance term w_c includes the disturbance term vector in relation (1A) u_p. Because of the negative sign on u_p, the coefficient estimates of Z_p are biased toward zero. This bias can be eliminated by instrumental variable (IV) estimates in which, based on substituting the relation obtained by lagging (1A) one generation into (1A), the great grandparental vector Z_{ggp} is used as instruments (note that Z_{ggp} would not provide eligible instruments for directly estimating relation (1) because of the multigenerationally correlated endowments in the compound disturbance term for relation (1), but are candidates for good instruments for relation (3) because the multigenerationally correlated endowments are not in the compound disturbance term for relation (3)).

Most of the many studies related to parental investments in children's human capital, the implications of such investments for distribution within the children's generation, and intergenerational mobility for LMICs do not deal with the estimation problems due to intergenerationally correlated endowments (or similarly intragenerationally correlated endowments for intragenerational mobility). But there are some that do, particularly through using instrumental variables or within-family estimates. These studies are emphasized in the reviews of studies in the next two sections. However it should be emphasized that such approaches may be heterogeneous in their quality. Just assuming some variable is a good instrument, for example, does not mean that in fact it predicts well the variable being instrumented and does not have direct effects on the second-stage outcome of interest in addition to any effect through the variable being instrumented. In addition even good instruments generally are likely to lead to local average treatment effects (LATE) for those affected by the instrument (e.g., those affected by a change in compulsory schooling regulations) or "compliers," and not average treatment effects for everyone.

3 Determinants of Children's Human Capital

Investments in children's human capital depend on decisions made initially primarily by parents but increasingly by children in light of household resources, composition, beliefs, markets (and market imperfections, such as for credit and information), policies (including provision of services supporting investments in human capital but also policies that affect expected returns to human capital investments). These investments in particular children determine those children's human capital, the nature of inequality within the children's generation, and the extent of *absolute* intergenerational and intragenerational mobility as indicated directly by human-capital measures themselves or by other outcomes determined importantly by these human capital measures such as earnings or income (Section 4). These investments in a generation of children in comparison with those in a particular child determine *relative* intergenerational and intragenerational mobility as indicated directly by the human-capital measures themselves or by other outcomes determined importantly by these human capital measures. The stronger are the intergenerational effects, the less is likely to be intergenerational relative mobility. In LMICs in comparison with HICs families are likely to play more important roles in these investments, even more so in more rural and remote areas, because of lesser development of market or public-sector institutions to support such human-capital investments, though such institutions have been developing rapidly in many LMICS and thus partially closing some of these gaps (Pollak, 1985). There also tend to be great data gaps between LMICs and HICs regarding information with which to analyze the determinants of human capital, some of which are noted below.

Recent series on early childhood development (ECD) in LMICs in *The Lancet* and elsewhere emphasize the critical role of early life in human-capital development, with the WHO Nurturing Care Framework (NCF) used to organize the discussion of the determinants of human capital in the 2017 series (Black et al., 2017; Britto et al., 2017; Black et al., 2021). The NCF has five components of enabling environments for child development: health, nutrition, security and safety, responsive caregiving, early learning. Figure 4 gives some of the activities related to each of these five components. As in Figure 1, families and policies and services play critical roles in determining these components of nurturing care in the early life stage and indirectly and directly in subsequent lifecycle stages for which the five components of the NCF framework are somewhat relabeled to be health, nutrition, security and safety, supportive relationships, learning opportunities (Black et al., 2021). I now review some studies on determinants of some critical child human capital outcomes.

Cognitive Skills

I begin with cognitive skills and what is presumed to be an important inputs into cognitive-skill production, schooling attainment, because that is the component of human capital that is thought to be most important and is most emphasized in the related empirical-economics literature. Cognitive-skill development begins in early life during the first two lifecycle stages in Figure 1, then continues during schooling ages in the third lifecycle stage and in the post-school ages in which learning occurs from experience as well as through training in the fourth and fifth lifecycle stages.

There are a small number of studies showing that negative shocks experienced in utero or in early life have persistent negative effects on child cognitive

Health	Nutrition	Security and Safety	Relationships and Responsive Caregiving	Learning Opportunities
• Disease prevention and treatment • Immunisations and well child visits • Water, sanitation, and hygiene	• Dietary diversity • Complementary food • Macronutrients and micronutrients • Breastfeeding	• Reduce adversities (abuse and neglect, violence) • Non institutional family care and early intervention for vulnerable children (e.g., disabled, malnourished, orphaned) • Birth registration	• Responsive parenting, feeding • Home visiting, parenting programmes • Caregiving routines • Support emotional development • Caregiver nurturance and continuity	• Continuity to primary school • Access to quality child care and preschool • Home opportunities to explore and learn • Books, toys, and play materials • Home visit, parenting

Figure 4 Nurturing care components for early life and preschool lifecycle stages
Source: Extracted and modified from Black et al. (2017), figure 1.

skills. Shocks from the disruptions and stresses caused by Chilean earthquakes when in early pregnancy have no significant effect on preschool children's cognition among middle-class families, but have strong negative influence among disadvantaged families, suggesting a critical role of family resources and endowments including parental human capital in buffering the impact of these negative shocks (Torche, 2018). Shocks from the dietary restrictions experienced in utero due to Ramadan in Indonesia are associated with lower scores on Raven's tests of nonverbal cognitive skills and math when children are 8–15 years of age, with stronger associations in lower quantiles and some differences between boys and girls (Majid, 2015; Majid et al., 2019). Similar effects of being in utero during Ramadan on children's cognitive achievement of 0.07–0.08 standard deviations at age seven are reported for Muslim minorities in HICs such as England (Almond et al., 2015). Since the vast majority of the world's 1.6 billion Muslims live in LMICs, this effect is likely to be much more important in LMICs than in HICs.

On the other hand negative rainfall shocks that are significantly associated with schooling attainment in Mexico (see below) are not associated with measures of earlier child cognitive skills (Adhvaryu et al., Forthcoming). For Nicaraguan boys of age 10, exposure to a conditional cash transfer (CCT) before age 2 appears critical for cognitive skills, though not for physical growth (Barham et al., 2013). Propensity score matching estimates, that are robust to a range of alternatives, of the impacts of measles vaccinations by ages 6–18 months to prevent the negative effects of the disease show cognitive and schooling benefits, as well as anthropometric benefits, in Ethiopia, India, and Vietnam (Nandi et al., 2019). Whether children are vaccinated, in turn, is significantly associated with parental schooling attainment and household wealth. Negative associations between early life adversities and adolescent IQ are lessened if there are subsequent childhood learning opportunities in Brazil and responsive caregiving in South Africa (Trude, 2021).

The massive primary school construction program in the 1970s in Indonesia has been analyzed to demonstrate substantial effects on schooling and subsequent labor market outcomes of children exposed to the program (Pitt et al., 1993; Duflo, 2001). A more recent study analyzes the effects of increased access to education in one generation on human capital outcomes in the form of cognitive skills in the next generation (Mazumder et al., 2019). Using longitudinal data, this study exploits the geographical and cohort variations in exposure to the Indonesian primary school expansion in 1973–1978 and finds, as did the earlier studies, that the school building project increased primary school completion rates among both men and women. The study also finds that children whose mothers were exposed to the 1970s school-building project score higher on the national primary-school examination, suggesting the importance of maternal education in the intergenerational transmission of human capital.

Based on a few influential studies, improved parenting developed through home visits or small mothers' groups and then subsequently preschool appear to be important factors in early life cognitive skills development, particularly for children from poorer family backgrounds (Engle et al., 2011; Cueto et al., 2016; Richter et al., 2017; Andrew et al., 2020; Grantham-McGregor et al., 2020). Despite the apparent potential for increasing human capital and absolute social mobility for children from poorer families through such programs, fairly strong socioeconomic gradients in preschool child cognitive skills by parental wealth, income, and schooling attainment begin at early ages and persist and in some cases enlarge by school-initiation ages (Fernald et al., 2011; Lopez-Boo, 2013; Schady et al., 2015; Reynolds et al., 2017a; Behrman et al., Forthcoming). Note that these studies generally do not use measures of parental cognitive skills to represent this dimension of parental human capital, but instead use an imperfect proxy in the form of one input into the production of cognitive skills, schooling attainment. However, the Chilean Survey of Early Infancy, a nationally representative longitudinal study of ~15,000 children under 5 years of age in 2010 (and followed up in 2012, 2018 and 2021), has rich data including indicators for maternal numeric and verbal cognitive skills. Analysis of these data finds that these maternal cognitive measures significantly predict early childhood cognitive and language skills for children ages 1–7 years even when controlling for the significant predictions of maternal schooling attainment (Abufhele-Milad, 2017). A separate study finds no robust significant association using alternative estimation methods (OLS with multiple controls, IV, PSM) between the proportion of time since birth that mothers have worked and cognitive skills of 3-year-olds (Reynolds et al., 2017b). Another study examines changes in household structure and finds that the presence of grandparents in extended households is associated with increased child performance on vocabulary tests and that the presence of fathers is associated with increased household income – but not with significant changes in preschool-age children's performance on cognitive tests (Reynolds et al., 2018). An after-school tutoring RCT in rural China, where many children are left-behind by parents (LBC) in care of grandparents, reports large home-tutoring reductions for non-LBC tutees but smaller reductions and larger test gains for LBC tutees (Behrman et al., 2022b). The extent of substitution of public for home tutoring, therefore, depends on household structure. Thus household structure in various ways, which is more likely to include extended families in LMICs than in HICs, may be an important aspect of how family background affects child development.

For school ages (lifecycle stage 3), there is some, but relatively limited, evidence pertaining to the determinants of child cognitive skills. For Argentina, there is quasi-experimental evidence that preschool programs increase basic school performance on standardized tests (Berlinski et al., 2009). Early life nutritional status (height-for-age z scores, HAZ), subsequent changes in HAZ, and better water and sanitation predict later childhood and adolescent performance on cognitive tests in the Young Lives longitudinal data for Ethiopia, India, Peru, and Vietnam (Crookston et al., 2013; Georgiadis et al., 2016; Dearden et al., 2017; Kowalski et al., 2018). HAZ in early life and to a lesser extent subsequent changes in HAZ, in turn, are predicted by parental resources, including parental schooling attainment (with variation in whether fathers' or mothers' schooling attainment has larger associations), parental household consumption, and maternal height (Schott et al., 2013). A separate study using the Young Lives data of the effects of mother adolescent undernutrition on offspring growth and development from infancy through adolescence using IV estimation that employs rainfall shocks during mothers' adolescence as instruments for mothers' nutritional status, however, finds no significant effect of mothers' adolescent nutritional status and rainfall shocks during mothers' adolescence on child achievement tests scores (Georgiadis et al., 2021). For the Philippines, estimates using sibling information to control for endogeneity find that that better-nourished children perform significantly better in school, partly because they enter school earlier and thus have more time to learn but mostly because of greater learning productivity per year of schooling, with a benefit-cost ratio of at least three (Glewwe et al., 2001). There does not seem to be a strong connection between early childhood nutrition and learning efforts, such as homework time and school attendance but they do find evidence that the primary-school enrollment of malnourished children tends to be delayed, probably because they are deemed unready for school at the minimum age of enrollment. The latter result on undernutrition delaying enrollment in primary schooling is also found for Ghana and for IV estimates for Pakistan (Alderman et al., 2001a; Glewwe et al., 2001). Conditional cash transfer (CCT) programs have widespread impacts on school attendance, on which they usually have been conditioned and school attainment, but there is mixed evidence on impacts on cognitive achievement (Todd and Wolpin, 2006; Fiszbein and Schady, 2009; Behrman et al., 2011; Behrman et al., 2013; Andersen et al., 2015; Sánchez et al., 2020; Behrman et al., 2021). When transfers to students and to teachers for learning mathematics in Mexican high schools were conditioned on levels and improvements in performance, however, fairly large (~0.60 SD) gains were found (Behrman et al., 2015). For rural China where over 60 million children are left-behind when parents migrate to urban areas for work, dynamic panel estimates that control for both unobserved individual heterogeneity and endogeneity in parental absence indicate that absence of both parents reduces children's contemporary cognitive achievements by 5.4 percentile points for math and 5.1 percentile points for Chinese (Zhang et al., 2014).

For post-school ages, there is some limited evidence. For Guatemala, estimates of production functions for adult verbal and nonverbal cognitive skills using data following individuals for ~35 years and treating the adult human capital as endogenous indicate that for adults 26–42 years of age: (1) School attainment has a significant and substantial effect on adult verbal cognitive skills but not on adult nonverbal cognitive skills; and (2) pre-school and post-school experiences also have substantial positive significant effects on adult cognitive skills (Behrman et al., 2014). Pre-school experiences captured by HAZ at 6 years are substantially and significantly associated with adult nonverbal cognitive skills, even after controlling for school attainment, indicating considerable human capital dynamic cross-complementarities. Post-school tenure in skilled jobs has significant positive effects on both types of cognitive skills. The findings (1) reinforce the importance of early life nutritional investments (see below); (2) support the importance of childhood nutrition and adult work complexity in explaining increases in nonverbal cognitive skills; (3) call into question interpretations of studies reporting productivity impacts of cognitive skills that do not control for endogeneity; and (4) point to limitations in using adult school attainment alone to represent human capital. In a related study using the same data set an experimentally allocated protein-enriched nutritional supplement during the first two years of life increased adult reading comprehension and nonverbal cognitive skills by about a quarter of a standard deviation for adults 26–42 years of age with no significant difference between men and women (Maluccio et al., 2009). Also parental schooling is significantly associated with cognitive skills when children are 26–42 years of age (Behrman et al., 2017a). Subsequently, these same individuals were followed in another data round when they were 38–55 years of age. Between young (26–42) and mature (38–55) adulthood (lifecycle stages 4 and 5), reading comprehension and nonverbal cognitive skills declined significantly in this sample for both males and females (Table 1) because of considerable aging during adulthood in such contexts. These changes point to the importance of taking age into account in characterizing either intergenerational or intragenerational social mobility in LMICs as indicated by cognitive skills. This point is well known in the literature on intergenerational mobility in HICs, but there the concern has been primarily about underestimating intergenerational persistence by using earnings and income estimates for young adults for which the current earning and income are likely to be quite noisy indicators of longer-run earning and income (Solon, 2002). Results from a few very different LMICs (Malawi, Mexico, South Africa) reinforce the point that age is important not only because of the fluctuations for young adults but also because cognitive skills change and often deteriorate with age (Avila et al., 2018; Kobayashi et al., 2018; Kohler et al., 2018; Soler-Hampejsek et al., 2018). In addition these studies suggest that schooling may play a mitigating role through reducing diabetes that is associated with cognitive decline in Mexico and that participation in the paid labor market may play a mitigating role at least for women in Malawi.

Though there are few studies on determinants of cognitive skills, there are many studies on a major input into cognitive skills, time in school, or schooling attainment. These studies regularly find significant relations between parental schooling attainment and child schooling attainment and in at least one study on rural China, about equal effects for co-resident grandparents (but not for non-coresident grandparents, which supports the interpretation that interaction with more-schooled grandparents is important instead of simply grandparental schooling being a proxy for other factors such as social class) (Zeng and Xie, 2014). Conventional wisdom is that the relations are stronger for mothers' schooling than for fathers' schooling, but a now-dated survey of 237 estimates reports larger coefficients for mothers' schooling than for fathers' schooling for relations with children's schooling as the dependent variables in only a little more than half of the studies (Behrman, 1997). Moreover fathers' schooling

Table 1 Means (SDs) for selected socioeconomic, cognitive and physical outcomes in young (26–42y) and mature (38–55y) adulthood in Guatemalan INCAP sample

	Men			Women		
	Young	**Mature**		**Young**	**Mature**	
Cognitive Outcomes						
Reading Comprehension, # correct out of 40	19.7	19.2	*	19.1	18.1	*
	(10.8)	(11.2)		(11.0)	(11.7)	
Cognitive Skills (Raven's) # correct out of 36	20.8	12.8	*	17.1	11.9	*
	(6.2)	(2.3)		(5.5)	(2.6)	
Physical Health Outcomes						
BMI, kg/m²	24.4	26.3	*	26.9	29.3	*
	(3.4)	(4.2)		(4.8)	(5.2)	
Overweight or obese, % BMI>25	39.2	61.7	*	62.5	78.8	*
Waist circumference, cm	86.3	93.4	*	92.3	101.9	*
	(9.0)	(10.5)		(12.0)	(12.3)	
Total cholesterol, mg/dL	158.3	179.0	*	166.7	191.1	*
	(32.3)	(39.6)		(31.7)	(38.8)	
Systolic blood pressure, mmHg	116.4	123.5	*	108.0	124.4	*
	(11.4)	(13.8)		(12.8)	(18.7)	
Diastolic blood pressure, mmHg	71.9	73.1	*	69.6	74.4	*
	(9.4)	(9.4)		(9.4)	(10.8)	

Pre-diabetes or diabetes, %	19.2	40.9	*	21.8	50.4	*
Pre-hypertension or hypertension, %	24.6	37.8	*	14.0	49.8	*
Metabolic syndrome, %	15.4	41.3	*	35.9	78.1	*
Current smoker, %	40.4	31.3	*	1.7	0.8	*

* Difference between young and mature adulthood significant at .05 level. Source: Author's calculations.

may be in part proxying for household income or wealth, so that its coefficient declines when wealth is included (Maluccio, 1998). Most of these studies are associational and cannot be given causal interpretations if there are intergenerationally correlated genetic and other endowments (see end of Section 2). At least one study for a HIC suggests that the failure to control for these endowments may affect substantially the estimated magnitudes of parental, particularly maternal, schooling in child schooling relations (Behrman and Rosenzweig, 2002). In this study the standard OLS estimates indicate significant positive coefficient estimates for mothers' and fathers' schooling, but when identical twins are used to control for shared common background including genetics at conception of parents, the coefficient estimates for mothers' schooling become significantly negative, which the authors interpret to reflect that in the context studied with controls for innate abilities and other factors, more-schooled women spend more time in the labor force and less time in child care. There are not significant effects on the estimated coefficients of fathers' schooling with the identical twins control in this study, consistent with fathers not adjusting their time spent with children at different schooling levels in that generation for the context studied. Some other studies also report substantial declines for the maternal schooling coefficient estimates in HICs with control for endogenous schooling choices using so-called "natural experiments" in the form of changes in minimum schooling requirements as instruments to break schooling-unobserved endowment correlations that otherwise bias upwards the coefficient estimate for maternal schooling (Black et al., 2005). Estimates using Chinese identical twins show similar patterns (Hu et al., 2021). OLS estimates show that one-year increases in maternal and parental schooling are associated, respectively, with 0.4 and 0.5 more years of children's schooling. However, with control for genetic and other endowment effects by using within-twins fixed effects and for measurement error using cross-twins reports, the results indicate that mothers' and fathers' schooling have no significant effects on children's schooling, results that are robust with various robustness checks. They suggest that the positive associations between children's and parents' schooling in standard cross-sectional estimates are mainly due to the correlation between parents' unobserved endowments and their schooling and not the effects of schooling per se. A study for Malaysia also finds that there is a common latent endowment component not only between parents' and their children's schooling but also with other relatives (Lillard and Kilburn, 1995).

Parents presumably invest in their children's schooling and other forms of human capital based on their perceived returns as reflected in the downward sloping lines in Figure 2. These perceptions may be inaccurate. Using survey data for eighth-grade boys in the Dominican Republic, a study finds that the perceived returns to secondary school are extremely low, despite high measured returns (Jensen, 2010). Students at randomly selected schools were given information on the higher measured returns completed on average 0.20–0.35 more years of school over the next four years than those who were not. This information effectively shifted the perceived rate of return to this human capital investment in Figure 2C from the dashed line to the solid line. A field experiment in Malawi finds that poor parents' baseline beliefs about their children's academic performance are inaccurate, but providing them with clear and digestible academic performance information causes them to update their beliefs and correspondingly adjust their investments: they increase school enrollments of their higher-performing children, decrease enrollments of their lower-performing children, and choose educational inputs that are more closely matched to their children's academic level (Dizon-Ross, 2019). The author suggests that these effects demonstrate the presence of important frictions preventing the use of available information, with heterogeneity analysis suggesting the frictions are worse among the poor. Thus the improved information effectively shifted the perceived rate of return to this human capital investment in Figure 2C from the dashed line to the solid line for higher-performing children and vice versa for lower-performing children. The results of these two studies suggest the importance of imperfect information markets in parental decisions to invest in their children's education. While the former study suggests that better information for poor parents is likely to increase human capital and social mobility for their children, the latter indicates that that is likely to be true only for the better-performing children and indeed the opposite might happen with poorer-performing children from poorer families. Of course for information to be effective, it has to be seen as relevant and credible by parents. It would seem therefore that information provided through the educational system might be more effective than information provided, for example, by researchers.

There is indirect evidence that imperfect capital markets may affect parental investments in their children in that, at least within the standard model in Figure 2; otherwise, parental resources per se would not affect the level of investments in children. Some studies find that parental resources are significant predictors of child schooling. For example, this result is found for the rural Philippines and for Vietnam, in both cases using panel data to control for unobserved endowments (Maluccio, 1998, Glewwe and Jacoby, 2004). A review of forty-two studies of child schooling for twenty-one countries reports that in about three-fifths of the cases income has a significant coefficient estimate, with a medium income elasticity of 0.07 (Behrman and Knowles, 1999). The same study reports estimates for Vietnam with an income elasticity about five times as large for grades completed per year and total grades completed, with somewhat larger effects for girls than for boys, if income is instrumented to control for measurement error and longer-run than annual parental resources are relevant for children's schooling decisions. However, this gross income estimate also incorporates the effects of parental schooling, which is among the instruments used. For Peru the progress through school is consistent with borrowing constraints being restraining for households that appear by their loan activity to be constrained in the capital market, but not for households that are not so constrained (Jacoby, 1994). Children from households with lower incomes, fewer durable assets, closer spacing for the next younger sibling, a male for the next older sibling, and greater sibling childcare responsibilities begin withdrawing from school earlier. In what the author claims is a stronger test the sample is split by low or high probability of being able to obtain loans under the (possibly strong) assumption that the sample split is based on exogenous variables and the coefficient estimates of the right-side variables are significant only for the more-constrained households and not the less-constrained households. For Malaysia there is evidence that children's schooling attainment is associated with their fathers' positions in the earnings cycle, suggesting the importance of credit constraints (Lillard and Kilburn, 1995). For rural India there is evidence that whether households are liquidity-constrained or not affects the time that mothers spend with their daughters (which presumably leads to greater cognitive stimulation), but not their sons (Rose, 2000). For Ghana, however, there is no significant evidence that borrowing constraints limit early school enrollment (Glewwe and Jacoby, 1993).

A small number of studies show that shocks experienced in utero or in early life have persistent effects on child schooling (in addition to those noted above that find effects on cognitive skills) in LMICs. Higher early life rainfall in Indonesia has positive effects on females, but not on males (Maccini and Yang, 2009). Females with 20 percent higher rainfall (relative to the local norm) complete 0.22 more schooling grades and live in households scoring 0.12 standard deviations higher on an asset index (the authors suggest that schooling attainment appears to mediate the impact on adult women's socioeconomic status). In Guatemala receiving a protein-enriched nutrient supplement when less than 2 or 3 years of age increased schooling attainment of adult women, but not men, by 1.2 schooling grades, about a fifth of the mean schooling for the generation affected (Maluccio et al., 2009). In Mexico, adverse rainfall in the year of birth decreases grade attainment, post-secondary enrollment, and employment outcomes, but children whose families were randomized to receive conditional cash transfers from PROGRESA experienced a much smaller decline: each additional year of program exposure during childhood mitigated more than 20 percent of early disadvantage (Adhvaryu et al., Forthcoming). The PROGRESA supplement to poor families' resources apparently facilitated offsetting the earlier adversity and induced greater investment in children's schooling attainment. In a pooled sample from Brazil, Guatemala, the Philippines, and South Africa, a unit increase in prenatal care utilization is significantly associated with 0.26 higher schooling grades attained (Liu et al., 2017).

Socioemotional Skills

Though there has been increased emphasis in the economic literature recently on the importance of socioemotional skills (in some cases referred to in the economic literature as "non-cognitive skills," though many psychologists object to that term because these skills are related to cognition), there are relatively few studies on the determinants of socioemotional skills in LMICS. Some of the studies noted above with regard to cognitive skills also tend to find that improved parenting developed through home visits or small mothers' groups appear to be important factors in early life socioemotional skills development, particularly for children from poorer family backgrounds (Engle et al., 2007; Engle et al., 2011; Cueto et al., 2016; Richter et al., 2017; Andrew et al., 2020; Grantham-McGregor et al., 2020). The study noted above that uses indicators for maternal numeric and verbal cognitive skills in addition to maternal schooling attainment for Chile and reports that these cognitive skills measures significantly predict early childhood cognitive and language skills for children ages 1–7 years even when controlling for the significant predictions of maternal schooling attainment also finds that the same for child socioemotional skills (Abufhele-Milad, 2017). However changes in household structure are not significantly associated with socioemotional skills in preschool-age Chileans, in contrast to the association with cognitive skills noted above (Reynolds et al., 2018). A study using a random sample of 2,617 adults aged 15–64 in thirteen urban areas in Colombia finds that higher levels of mothers' schooling attainment significantly predict better scores on adults' (1) extroversion and openness to experience, (2) emotional stability and hostile attribution bias, and (3) conscientiousness, grit and decision making (Acosta et al., 2015).

Health and Nutritional Status

It is widely thought that the first 1,000 days after conception is a critical period (lifecycle stage 1 in Figure 1) and some influential studies claim that the window of opportunity is virtually closed after 24/36 months of age (Victora et al., 2008; Victora et al., 2010). Birthweight is the most readily available and most commonly used indicator of prenatal factors, though in a few cases other measures (e.g., gestational age, low birthweight, birthweight relative to gestational age, prematuriy, birth length, APGAR scores) are used. Low birthweight (<2500 gm) is widespread in many LMICs, particularly in South Asia with prevalence of 27 percent, with sub-Saharan Africa and the Middle East and North Africa next in the 11–14 percent range and Latin America, East Asia and the Pacific, Europe and Central Asia, and North America in the 6–9 percent range (Table 2).

Stunting (HAZ < 2 SD below medians for well-nourished populations) is the primary indicator of chronic undernourishment used. About a quarter of the world's children under 5 years of age are stunted, with prevalences of ~33 percent in sub-Saharan Africa and South Asia, all much higher than the 2.5 percent that would be expected in a well-nourished population (Table 2). The number of children under 5 years of age who are stunted, though declining from 253 million in 1990, still is enormous, 171.4 million in 2010 and 142 million in 2020 (de Onis et al., 2011). While prevalence of stunting has declined secularly in recent decades, the prevalence of overweight/obesity has increased rapidly; among children under 5 years of age, the numbers overweight/obese rose from 26.9 million in 1990 to 42.8 million in 2010 and 59.4 million in 2020, 84 percent of whom are in LMICs (de Onis et al., 2010). Thus many LMICs are characterized as having a double burden of malnutrition – persistent, though declining, chronic undernutrition and rapidly expanding overnutrition. Though systematic data are less available for older ages, the prevalence of overweight/ obesity appears much higher than for children under 5 and increasing over the lifecycle. A recent study examines trajectories in stunting and overweight from age 1 year to mid-adolescence and from mid-childhood to early adulthood among two cohorts using the Young Lives data from Ethiopia, India, Peru, and Vietnam (Schott et al., 2019). Group-based trajectory analysis with five ages of overweight and stunting for each country-cohort reveals (1) trajectories of catch-up growth for a subset of study children between the ages of 12 and 19 in the older cohort in Ethiopia (20.1 percent of the cohort), India (20.5 percent), Peru (16.9 percent) and Vietnam (14.0 percent); (2) trajectories of increasing probabilities of stunting as children age from 12 to 22 in the older cohort in India (22.2 percent) and Peru (30.7 percent); (3) trajectories of childhood increases in

Table 2 Prevalences of low birthweight and stunting by major world regions

	Low birth weight: % of live births < 2500 gm in 2015 (updated May 2019)	**Stunting (moderate and severe):** % of children in 2018 aged 0-59 months < 2 SD below medians for WHO standards for well-nourished populations (updated March 2019)
Sub-Saharan Africa	14	33.3
Middle East and North Africa	11.3	14.7
South Asia	27	34.4
East Asia and the Pacific	7.9	8.4
Latin America & Caribbean	8.8	9
Europe & Central Asia	6.9	9
North America	7.9	2.6

Sources: (downloaded August 12, 2019): https://data.unicef.org/resources/resource-type/datasets/# https://data.unicef.org/resources/dataset/malnutrition-data/

overweight probabilities (younger cohort: India, 3.4 percent, Peru, 19.4 percent and Vietnam, 8.1 percent) and of later (adolescent) increases in overweight probabilities (older cohort: Ethiopia, 0.5 percent, India, 6.3 percent, Peru, 40.9 percent, and Vietnam, 9.4 percent). Multinomial logit prediction of membership in trajectory categories reveals that higher wealth quartiles and maternal schooling are protective against high-stunting-probability-trajectory-group membership, but higher wealth and urban residence predict high-overweight-probability-trajectory-group membership. This evidence suggests a window of opportunity for interventions to reduce stunting and to avert overweight development in adolescence, in addition to the often-emphasized first 1,000 days after conception. Another study using the Young Lives data investigates relations between household conditional wealth (i.e., wealth at age 15 not predicted by wealth at age 5, thus controlling for wealth at age 5 and any correlated factors) and child height at age 15 utilizing longitudinal data on 7150 children (Duc, 2019). This study finds two dimensions of heterogeneity: (1) The effect of conditional wealth on adolescent height is stronger for boys than for girls, which is striking because a number of studies reviewed in this section report that girls tend to benefit more at the margin from positive changes. (2) Growth of children after age 5 who were stunted at that age is significantly more responsive to conditional wealth than the growth of non-stunted children. For Nicaraguan boys of age 10, exposure to a CCT before age 2 does not appear critical for physical growth due to subsequent catch-up, though it does appear critical for cognitive skills (Barham et al., 2013). Table 1 shows substantially increasing overweight/obesity between young and mature adulthood in the Guatemalan INCAP study referred to above, reaching 61.7 percent for men and 78.8 percent for women in the 38- to 55-year-old age range, as well as increases in a number of other indicators of related health problems (e.g., high blood pressure, cholesterol, prediabetic/diabetic, metabolic syndrome).

Prenatal care is emphasized by the World Health Organization (WHO) and others as critical for birth outcomes, and the extent of prenatal care tends to be associated with parental education and other resources. However, prenatal-care utilization is not significantly associated with birthweights in a pooled sample from Brazil, Guatemala, the Philippines, and South Africa, but a unit increase in prenatal care utilization is significantly associated with 0.09 higher HAZ at 24 months (and, as noted above, more schooling grades attained) (Liu et al., 2017). Although there is some heterogeneity and greater imprecision across sites, the results are qualitatively similar among the four different populations. On the other hand, fixed-effects analysis of monthly panel with all births in Mexico from 2008 to 2010 merged with homicide data at the municipality level finds that exposure to homicides in the first trimester of gestation increases infant birthweight and reduces the proportion of low birthweights (Torche and Villarreal, 2014). The authors suggest that the mechanism driving this surprising positive effect is an increase in mothers' health-enhancing behaviors (particularly the use of prenatal care) as a result of exposure to violence. The positive effect of homicide exposure is heterogeneous across SES: strong among low-SES women living in urban areas – and null among the most advantaged women. This variation suggests that behavioral responses to an increase in local homicides depend on a combination of increased vulnerability and access to basic resources that allow women to obtain prenatal care. Also there is some evidence that birthweight is related to parental SES. For example, there is a positive significant association between whether mother has finished lower secondary education and birthweight in Vietnam, though the positive association with the family wealth index is not significant (Duc and Behrman, 2017). In China, higher pollution is associated with lower birthweights, but this association is mitigated for children whose mothers have higher schooling attainment (Liu et al., 2022). In the Young Lives longitudinal data for Ethiopia, India, Peru, and Vietnam, HAZ in early life and to a lesser extent subsequent changes in HAZ, in turn, are predicted by parental resources, including parental schooling attainment (with variation in whether fathers' or mothers' schooling attainment has larger associations), parental household consumption, and maternal height (Schott et al., 2013). For rural India there is evidence that favorable rainfall shocks in childhood increase the survival probabilities of girls to a greater extent than they increase boys' survival probabilities and that price shocks have greater impact on girls than on boys, both of which suggest families treat girls more as luxuries at the margin when there are real income changes (Behrman and Deolalikar, 1990; Rose, 1999).

Production function estimates for height and weight growth for children between 6 and 24 months old in Guatemala and the Philippines, using instrumental variables to control for endogeneity and estimating multiple specifications, find that protein intake plays an important and positive role in height and weight growth (Puentes et al., 2016). Energy from other macronutrients, however, does not have robust relations with these two anthropometric measures. A recent systematic review using meta-analysis techniques shows that while the average impact of income transfers from social-protection programs on HAZ is positive, effect sizes are small and not statistically significant (Manley et al., 2013). If households use these transfers largely to increase the quantity of calories consumed, if the increases in protein consumption is small in magnitude, or if these proteins are not allocated to the target children, then these production function results suggest that such transfers will have little impact on these children's heights – precisely what the review finds. Another recent study also finds no impacts of Green Revolution–induced increases in rice productivity on children's HAZ (Headey and Hoddinott, 2016), also consistent with the production function estimates and small protein elasticities with respect to income. These studies suggest that interventions designed to increase household incomes may only improve children's nutritional status when they are linked to mechanisms that also improve the quality of children's diets. Such interventions, e.g., linking nutritional behavior-change communication (BCC) to social-protection interventions or "nutrition-sensitive agriculture," await further study. Estimates of parental allocation decisions regarding proteins in the Guatemalan context indicate fairly small income elasticities but that the reference population for the distribution of HAZ that parents use is important and that parents use the local distribution of HAZ for 2-year-olds in making their decisions regarding proteins to feed their newborn children over the first two years of their lives (Wang et al., Forthcoming). Indeed in the six years after the equivalent of a 38 percent price subsidy was introduced experimentally, almost half of the HAZ gains for those who receive the subsidy are due to the reference-point effect and the rest to the price subsidy. The structural behavioral model also suggests that if parents used the distribution of heights for well-nourished children, that arguably represents the true potential for their children, rather than the local distribution, then they would invest significantly more in the protein intake of their children and the distribution of the heights of their children would be significantly higher. This would be tantamount to moving from the dashed to the solid line in Figure 2C with better information markets. A study on Bangladesh provides further insight on the role of nutritional knowledge and finds that maternal nutritional knowledge, instrumented to control for endogeneity and measurement error, has significant impact on children's dietary diversity if and only if the household has good market access, illustrating one way in which context matters (Hirvonen et al., 2017).

There is an emerging literature, mostly still in the working paper stage and mostly on HICs, on the role of parental beliefs about the technology for producing child outcomes (e.g., Cunha et al. 2013; Boneva and Rauh, 2018; Attanasio et al., 2019; Bhalotra et al., 2020). A few of these studies are on LMICs. A 2019 study on Colombia, for example, considers an 18-month-long parenting stimulation program targeted to 1,429 children aged 12–24 months at baseline from low-income households (Attanasio et al., 2019). In this program, home visitors visited weekly to randomly chosen households to improve mother-child interactions and other maternal behaviors to foster children's cognitive and socioemotional skills. This study finds that mothers' subjective beliefs predict investments in their children (but that the program did not affect mothers' subjective beliefs) and that mothers underestimate the returns to their investments in their children. A 2020 study on 1,100 mothers who recently gave birth in rural Pakistan, for another example, explores the relevance of subjective expectations of returns to and effort costs of breastfeeding and stimulation (Bhalotra et al., 2020). This study finds heterogeneity across mothers in expected effort costs and expected returns for outcomes in cognitive, socio-emotional, and health domains and shows that these heterogeneities in beliefs about returns and costs are associated with heterogeneities in investments in children.

A 2017 study analyzes the relation between parental schooling and stunting using 376,992 preschool children from 56 LMICs (Alderman and Headey, 2017). It compares a naïve OLS model to specifications that include cluster fixed effects and cohort-based educational rankings to attempt to reduce biases from omitted variables and finds that the estimated nutritional effects of parental schooling are: (a) substantially reduced in models that include fixed effects and cohort rankings; (b) larger for mothers than for fathers particularly for higher schooling levels (e.g., > 10 grades); (c) minimal for primary schooling but generally increasing with more schooling; (d) increasing with household wealth; (e) larger in countries/regions with higher burdens of undernutrition; (f) larger in countries/regions with higher schooling quality; and (g) highly variable across country sub-samples. The authors conclude that these results imply substantial uncertainty and variability in the returns to education, but their more stringent models imply that even the achievement of very ambitious schooling targets would only lead to modest reductions in stunting rates in high-burden countries, and they speculate that schooling might have more impact on the nutritional status of the next generation if school curricula focused on directly improving health and nutritional knowledge of future parents.

There is much less literature investigating the determinants of physical well-being for older children in LMICs, especially with control for endogeneity and unobserved parental endowments that are likely to bias cross-sectional estimates. But there are some studies. For rural India, for example, there are estimates of parental preferences underlying intrahousehold allocations of nutrients among children up to 13 years of age using the SET model discussed above with regard to Figure 3 with control for unobserved family endowments (Behrman, 1988a; Behrman, 1988b). These estimates find (1) important seasonal differences, with greater inequality aversion in the surplus season when food is relatively abundant than in the lean season when food is scarce, (2) a promale bias of about 5 percent in the lean season that is larger for lower castes and households with more-educated household heads (but not related to land holdings), (3) significant birth-order effects favoring lower birth orders and (4) significant inequality aversion but less than found in studies for the United States, particularly in the lean season, which implies that more vulnerable children (e.g., girls, higher birth order) are particularly at risk when food is most scarce. For China there is a study that builds on the extension of the same model and uses identical twins of average age 11 years to control for unobserved endowments (Yi et al., 2015). This study finds that in response to health shocks, parents make compensatory and reinforcing investments in different dimensions of human capital across children. Compared with the twin sibling who did not suffer from negative early health shocks at age 0–3, the other twin sibling who did received 305 yuan more health investment, but received 182 yuan less educational investment. The study concludes that overall families acts as net equalizers in response to early health shocks across children. A study using the Young Lives data for Ethiopia, India, Peru, and Vietnam of the effects of mothers' adolescent undernutrition on offspring growth and development using IV estimation that employs rainfall shocks during mothers' adolescence as instruments for mothers' nutritional status finds significant effects of mothers' adolescent nutritional status and rainfall shocks during mothers' adolescence on child height-for-age in infancy that persists through to adolescence (though, as noted above, no significant affects on child achievement tests scores) (Georgiadis et al., 2021).

I have not been able to find systematic studies in LMICs of the role of parental education and endowments in the determinants of children's mental health.

4 Impacts of Children's Human Capital

Children's human capital is of interest in itself because it relates to the children's welfare and capabilities. But it also is of interest because it may affect other outcomes, such as occupations, income, and social mobility. There are definite empirical challenges in LMICs for assessing the impacts of human capital, pertaining to measurement (quality of investments, unobserved endowments, simultaneity) and data related to the framework above. In future data collection it would be desirable to undertake longitudinal studies in more LMIC contexts with rich measurements of human capital and human capital investments and with links to administrative price and service data that would permit using quasi-experimental methods to understand better the investment responses and to control for endogeneities. Linking to administrative data on human capital outcomes, such as test scores and health status, has been increasing and hopefully can be further increased.

Despite such challenges, there are some longitudinal studies among children exposed to poverty and other adverse conditions in specific LMIC contexts that show beneficial effects of early life interventions on adult wage earnings (Hoddinott et al., 2008; Gertler et al., 2014), competence (e.g., intelligence quotient, educational attainment and general knowledge) (Maluccio et al., 2009; Walker et al., 2011), reductions in violence, depressive symptoms and social inhibition (Walker et al., 2011), and growth in the subsequent generation (Behrman et al., 2009; Walker et al., 2015). Benefit-cost ratios based on long-run impacts on earnings are estimated to be in the 6.4–17.6 range for increasing preschool enrollment rates for poorer children toward those for children from households in the top quintiles and in the 3.5–47.9 range for reducing stunting in high prevalence countries (Engle et al., 2011; Hoddinott et al., 2013a). These and related findings are widely interpreted to provide economic justification for investment in early childhood, especially in children younger than 3 years of age (Doyle et al., 2009; Hoddinott et al., 2013a; Richter et al., 2017) . They also are interpreted to imply that the so-called Heckman Curve (Heckman, 2006) with declining rates of return to human capital investments in children as they age probably holds in LMICs. Of course if there are diminishing marginal returns to such investments, this curve presumably is a disequilibrium relation that will flatten out if investments are directed to the currently disequilibrium highest rate-of-return investments.

Cognitive Skills

Cognitive skills are of interest in themselves as important forms of human capital, as well as possible outcomes for comparison across generations to measure intergenerational mobility or across ages to measure intragenerational mobility, though I am not aware of studies that make such comparisons for LMICs. They also are of interest as possible determinants of other outcomes, such as income and occupation, which are indicators often used for studies of welfare and of social mobility. Again I am aware only of a very few studies that estimate such relations for LMICs and attempt to control for the endogeneity of cognitive skills. One example for Guatemala reports significant positive effects of adult cognitive skills on wages using instruments from over 35 years of the lifecycle including early life experimentally allocated nutritional supplements to treat cognitive skills and a measure of physical human capital (fat-free mass) as endogenous. This study finds significant and substantial effects for cognitive skills (about two-thirds larger in the IV than in OLS estimates), but not for the physical human capital measure even in a fairly poor agrarian economy (except for a subsample selected into physically intensive occupations) (Behrman et al., 2017a).

Another study, though it does not attempt to control for endogeneity, controls for selectivity regarding who receives earnings and presents quantile estimates using measures of cognitive (literacy assessment) and socioemotional skills (Five Factor Model skills of extraversion, agreeableness, conscientiousness, neuroticism and openness, as well as measures of grit, hostile-attribution bias, decision-making, risk aversion and time preference) to examine how schooling and skills differences between men and women relate to gender gaps in earnings using data on adults aged 25–54 years from the 2012–13 World Bank Skills toward Employment and Productivity (STEP) program for nine middle-income countries: Armenia, Bolivia, Colombia, Georgia, Ghana, Kenya, Serbia, Ukraine, and Vietnam (Gunewardena et al., 2018). This analysis finds that post-secondary schooling and cognitive skills are more important for women's earnings at the lower end and middle of the earnings distribution. Especially at the lower end of the earnings distribution, women are disadvantaged not so much by having lower human capital than men, but by institutional factors such as wage structures that reward women's human capital systematically less than men's.

There are many – hundreds, if not thousands – studies that consider the associations of schooling attainment, an input into the production of cognitive skills, with a range of outcomes in LMICs. Some of these are reviewed above with regard to the impact of parental schooling on children's human capital. Many of these in the economics literature focus on wages or earnings as the outcome of interest (Psacharopoulos and Patrinos, 2004). But most of these are simply OLS associations that do not control for possible (1) measurement error (which, if random, tends to bias the estimates toward zero) or (2) unobserved endowments such as genetic ability or family background that are likely to affect schooling and the outcome of interest in addition to any effects through schooling (which are likely to bias OLS coefficients away from zero). There is a fairly large literature for HICs that attempts to control for these biases, with results that suggest biases in both directions, though often with the unobserved-variable biases dominating so OLS estimates overestimate schooling effects. There are many fewer studies for LMICS, a few examples of which I now note. For urban China, a study estimates a wage relation using twins data to control for unobserved endowments and cross-twins schooling reports to control for measurement error (Li et al., 2012). Their OLS estimates suggest that one year of schooling increases an individual's earnings by 8.4 percent. Their within-twins fixed-effects estimates are 2.7 percent, but rise to 3.8 percent after the correction for measurement error. These results suggest that a large portion of the estimated returns to education using OLS methods is due to omitted ability or the family effect. They further investigate why the true return is low and the omitted ability bias high and find evidence showing that it may be a consequence of China's highly selective and exam-oriented educational system. More specifically, they find that high-school education may mainly serve as a mechanism to select college students, but as a human-capital investment per se it has low earnings returns. Another study for urban China using these same twins data investigates the impact of schooling on health-related behaviors and outcomes (Behrman et al., 2015). OLS estimates suggest that schooling is significantly associated with adult health-related behaviors (smoking, drinking, exercising) but not with own or spouse health outcomes (general health, mental health, overweight, chronic diseases). However, within-identical-twins estimators change the estimates for approximately half of these health indicators, in one case declining in absolute magnitude and becoming insignificant and in the other cases increasing in absolute magnitudes. Within-MZ estimates indicate significant pro-health effects for at least one of the indicators for own health (better mental health), own health-related behaviors (less smoking) and spouse health (less overweight). For the rural Philippines, in contrast, using panel data to provide relevant instruments (particularly distance to schools and measures of household resources at the time of schooling) to endogenize investments in schooling in wage functions, the estimated return to schooling increases more than 60 percent when schooling is endogenized, suggesting the dominance of measurement error and increasing returns to higher schooling in OLS estimates (Maluccio, 1998).

Socioemotional Skills

There is increasing evidence that socioemotional skills (some times referred to as "noncognitve skills"), have important economic outcomes, perhaps in some contexts more important than cognitive skills, in HICs (Heckman et al., 2006; Cunha and Heckman, 2008). There is fairly limited, though recently increasing, evidence for LMICs in studies that consider both cognitive and socioemotional skills.

Analysis of longitudinal data on rural children from one of China's poorest provinces finds that both cognitive and socioemotional skills, measured when children are 9–12, 13–16, and 17–21 years old, are important predictors of whether they remain in school or enter the workforce at age 17–21 (Glewwe et al., 2017). The predictive power of specific skill variables differ between boys and girls. Conditioning on grades of schooling attained, there is no strong evidence that skills measured in childhood predict wages in the early years of labor-market participation.

Another study finds that both cognitive and socioemotional skills matter for favorable labor-market outcomes in Colombia, though with distinct roles (Acosta et al., 2015). Cognitive skills are strongly associated with higher earnings and holding formal jobs or high-qualified occupations. In contrast, socioemotional skills appear to have little direct influence on these outcomes but play stronger roles in labor-market participation. Both types of skills, especially cognitive, are strongly associated with tertiary education. These inferences are generally consistent across types of estimates for approaches using both disaggregated measures of skills (OLS, logit, and IV) and aggregated measures (structural estimations of latent skills).

For Argentina and Chile, another study based on cross-sectional data for young adults in their late 20s finds that self-efficacy is the ability that predominates in the association with higher wages, with stronger effects for workers with postsecondary degrees (Bassi et al., 2012). Self-efficacy also is the socioemotional skill most associated with higher labor-force participation and the probabilities of being employed.

A recent study for Peru estimates the returns to cognitive and socioemotional skills using a labor-force survey designed to measure these skills in the working-age (14–50 years old) urban population (Díaz et al., 2012). The survey measures a wide range of cognitive (Peabody receptive language, verbal fluency, working memory, and numeracy/problem – solving) and personality traits to proxy for socioemotional skills (Big – Five Factors, Grit). Both types of skills are significant correlates of earnings. Using instrumental variables to address the potential endo-geneity of measured skills vis-à-vis schooling, the findings indicate that socio-emotional and cognitive skills are equally valued in the Peruvian labor market. A one standard-deviation change in an overall cognitive skill measure and in the perseverance facet of Grit each generates a 9 percent increase on average earnings, conditional on schooling. The effect of an increase in schooling of about 3 grades is a 15 percent increase in earnings, conditional on skills. The returns to other socioemotional skills vary across dimensions of personality: 5 percent higher earnings for emotional stability and 8 percent lower earnings for agreeableness.

A study using linked employer-employee data from the formal sector of Bangladesh explores gender wage gaps associated with measures of cognitive skills and personality traits (Nordman et al., 2015). The results are that while cognitive skills are important in determining mean wages, personality traits have little explanatory power. However, quantile regressions indicate that personality traits do matter in certain parts of the conditional wage distribution, especially for wages of females. Cognitive skills as measured by reading and numeracy also confer different benefits across the wage distribution to females and males respectively. Quantile decompositions indicate that these skills and traits reduce the unexplained gender gap, mainly in the upper parts of the wage distribution.

A study mentioned above presents quantile estimates using measures of cognitive and socioemotional skills (Five Factor Model skills of extraversion, agreeableness, conscientiousness, neuroticism, and openness, as well as meas-ures of grit, hostile attribution bias, decision-making, risk aversion, and time preference) to examine how schooling and skills differences between men and women relate to gender gaps in earnings using data on adults aged 25–54 years from the 2012–13 World Bank STEP program for nine middle-income coun-tries: Armenia, Bolivia, Colombia, Georgia, Ghana, Kenya, Serbia, Ukraine, and Vietnam (Gunewardena et al., 2018). This analysis finds that men and women have positive returns to openness to new experiences and risk-taking behaviors and negative returns to hostile-attribution bias.

Health and Nutritional Status

There is some evidence on the effects of physical health and nutritional status, though there is a question of to what extent the indicators used are proxying for other factors such as early life cognitive development or age of entering adolescence. I have not been able to locate, however, systematic evidence on the effects of mental health on relevant outcomes in LMICs.

Table 3 presents estimates of the gains over the lifecycle from moving a child out of low birthweight status based on estimates that the authors deemed were the best available estimates for low-income countries (Alderman and Behrman, 2006). Since many of these gains, particularly in adult productivities, are

Modified by author from Alderman and Behrman (2006).

decades after birth, the choice of discount rates is important. With a moderate discount rate (5 percent) the majority of these estimated gains are from increased adult productivities, not the relatively short-run gains in infancy that have been emphasized in much of the previous biomedical literature (though this depends critically on how averted mortality is valued). Estimates of benefit-cost ratios using these impacts range from 0.6 to 35.2 (Behrman et al., 2004). Thus for a number of interventions to reduce low birthweight, these estimates suggest attractive investment possibilities, substantially due to productivity gains in lifecycle stages 4 and 5 in response to investments in lifecycle stage 1 due to dynamic complementarities with early life nutrition.

For Chile, birthweight differences within twins pairs, which control for all the unobserved family and genetic background factors that the twins have in

Table 3 Estimates of present discounted values of seven major benefits of moving one infant out of low-birth-weight status, at different discount rates (U.S. dollars), in low-income country

	Annual Discount Rate		
	3%	5%	10%
1. Reduced infant mortality	94	93	89
2. Reduced neonatal care	42	42	42
3. Reduced costs of infant and child illness	36	35	34
4. Productivity gain from reduced stunting	152	85	25
5. Productivity gain from increased cognitive ability	367	205	60
6. Reduced costs of chronic diseases	49	15	1
7. Intergenerational benefits	92	35	6
Total	832	510	257

Source: Author's table based on Alderman and Behrman (2006)

common and factors that may differential families with twins from other families, have no effects on cognitive scores for children under 3 years of age, positive effects for children 3–7 years of age and substantial effects on first graders' math and fourth graders' math and language test scores (Torche and Echevarría, 2011; Abufhele-Milad, 2017). The within-twins estimates also include significant effects of birthweight on early life anthropometrics (WAZ, HAZ) and significant associations of WAZ with cognitive and HAZ with socio-emotional indicators.

For the Philippines, estimates using sibling information for instruments (which results in substantially larger estimates than OLS) find that better-nourished children at the time of initial enrollment decisions perform significantly better in school at age ~11 years, partly because they enter school earlier and thus have more time to learn but mostly because of greater learning productivity per year of schooling, with particularly large effects for more undernourished children (Glewwe et al., 2001). These estimates imply that a unit increase in HAZ would have effects on student achievement equal to 1.1 grades of school (2.1 grades for the most undernourished children) with a benefit-cost ratio of at least 3. For Pakistan, estimates using price shocks as instruments (which results in substantially larger estimates than OLS) find fairly substantial reductions in starting age for schools with higher preschool HAZ, larger for girls than for boys (Alderman et al., 2001b). For Ghana, preschool undernutrition also results in significant schooling delays (Glewwe and Jacoby, 1993). For rural India, propensity score matching estimates using longitudinal data from a controlled protein-energy supplement nutrition trial conducted near Hyderabad in 1987 to 1990 reports that in 2003–2005 children born in intervention villages are 7.8 percent more likely to be enrolled in school and complete 0.84 (95 percent CI: 0.28, 1.39; P < 0.005) more schooling grades than children born in control villages, but no association between supplementary nutrition and academic performance, as measured by school test scores (Nandi et al., 2016). Thus these estimates suggest that there are significant dynamic cross productivities between preschool nutrition and schooling achievement, illustrating how the effects of better early life nutrition in lifecycle stages 1 and 2 in Figure 1 affect school-age cognitive and schooling outcomes in lifecycle stage 3, which in turn are likely to affect adult outcomes in lifecycle stages 4 and 5.

Estimates using the Guatemalan INCAP data with an experimentally allocated protein-enhanced supplement versus an alternative proteinless supplement for children under 24 months of age indicates long-run mostly positive significant effects over the lifecycle, thereby linking lifecycle stage 1 in Figure 1 with lifecycle stages 3–5 through increasing schooling for by over a grade for females, increasing adult reading comprehension and cognitive abilities by about a quarter of a standard deviation for both adult men and women, increasing hourly wage rates for men by over 40 percent and increasing birthweights for children of women who received the supplements by over 100 gm (Hoddinott et al., 2008; Behrman et al., 2009; Maluccio et al., 2009). These estimates again suggest attractive investment possibilities, substantially due to productivity gains in lifecycle stages 4 and 5 in response to investments in lifecycle stage 1 due to dynamic complementarities with early life nutrition.

A study using Chinese twins data to control for endowments finds impacts of birthweight on schooling attainment, cognitive achievement as measured by ninth-grade language and math tests and wages (Rosenzweig and Zhang, 2013). These effects are significantly larger for females than for males, which the authors interpret to reflect a comparative advantage of females in more-skilled occupations together with a shift toward skill-intensive occupations associated with economic growth.

5 Implications of Estimates Such as Summarized in Sections 3 and 4 for Inequality and Poverty in the Children's Generation

The relations between parental human capital and endowments and children's human capital, in addition to the implications for children's human capital, clearly are related to inequality and poverty in the children's generation. But there is limited evidence from LMICs on these implications of the estimates. I review three studies that investigate the impacts of changes on distribution in the children's generation through conditional cash transfers (CCTs), the receipt of which depends on parental income being below a poverty cutoff and through improving parental schooling and income on the poverty and income distribution of the children's generation.

Effects of Mexican Oportunidades CCT Program on Schooling Attainment, Height and Distribution of Future Earnings

This study develops and applies a nonparametric simulation method to study how this CCT program affects the distribution of earnings for the children's generation when they become adults (McKee and Todd, 2011). In this program, families receive transfers if they are below the poverty line and satisfy conditions related to children's health and school attendance, so the program may affect the earnings distribution through increasing children's schooling attainment and height, as a measure of long-term nutritional status. The findings suggest that human-capital investments in today's youth will increase their mean earnings levels, but will have only a modest effect on earnings inequality.

The key factors underlying the modest effects on inequality are the difficulty in predicting which children will become future low-earning adults and nonlinearities in how health and education are priced in the labor market. With regard to the first factor, childhood poverty is a strong predictor of future low earnings, but there is also substantial intergenerational mobility that makes it difficult to target low adult earners on the basis of childhood characteristics. With regard to the second factor, this study finds evidence of important nonlinearities in how height and education influence earnings. Most notably, an additional year of secondary school has a higher monetary return than an additional year of primary school. Because of these nonlinearities, people at the upper deciles of the targeted population tend to benefit more from the program intervention. The authors note some limitations of the simulation method used: (1) Their method assumes that the observed relationships between earnings and the covariates of education, height, and work experience are causal, which raises concern about potential biases due to unobserved abilities. (2) The characteristics of today's 25- to 40-year-olds, observed in 2002, are assumed to be representative of the future adulthood of today's children. (3) The method does not account for the general-equilibrium effects of increasing schooling levels of a large segment of the future labor force, which probably would tend to decrease returns to schooling through expanding the supplies of more-schooled individuals, though there may be somewhat offsetting expansions of demands for such individuals through induced consumption changes. (4) This study focused on individual earnings for men and women, although household-level earnings inequality may be more relevant to policymakers.

Simulations of Impacts of Increasing Schooling Attainment and Income of Poor Parents on Distributions of Children's Cognitive and Health Outcomes in Young Lives' Countries Of Ethiopia, India, Peru, and Vietnam

Theoretical models, empirical estimates, and policy prescriptions place considerable emphasis on the importance of families and their roles in improving life chances of children, with early childhood ages of particular importance. A widely held perception is that improving schooling attainment and income/consumption for parents in poor households will substantially improve living standards in the current generation and improve the human capital accumulated among their children and, consequently, reduce poverty and inequality in the next generation of adults This study's (Behrman et al., 2017b) aim is to examine whether attaining specific targets (such as decreasing the proportion of people living on less than

$1 a day and or ensuring primary-school completion as targeted by the Millennium Development Goals) in the parental generation would result in substantial reductions in poverty and inequality in their children's generation. The study finds that changing parental schooling to at least the primary level does little to change the prevalence of poverty, as measured by the proportion below some cutoff and inequality in the distribution of parental schooling. Increasing parental schooling much more to a minimum of nine grades, however, reduces inequality in terms of parental schooling considerably but results in little change in poverty (again in the sense of the proportion below some cutoff) and very little change in the inequality of the distribution of the human capital of their children. The same is true if per capita consumption of parents is raised to a minimum of $1 a day or to the 20th percentile of the per-capita-consumption distribution. Were the Millennium Development Goal of universal primary education achieved, it would imply some fifty-seven million additional children of primary-school age in developing regions attending school (United Nations Development Program, 2014). This would be an important gain. However, it is likely that even in this scenario, substantial inequality in human capital would remain. To some, it may seem trivial that inequalities remain, since even in these hypothetical scenarios, the parents at the bottom of the distribution remain at the bottom (albeit at a higher level). However, for the parents of Young Lives children to have met this Millennium Development Goal would have implied an additional one to three grades on average per parent with less than primary schooling; to have achieved the goal of a universal nine grades of schooling would have implied an additional five to seven grades of schooling per Young Lives parent. These are very large increases as compared, for example, with the estimated impacts of about 0.7 grades of the very visible Mexican CCT program (Schultz, 2004; Behrman et al., 2005). The latter scenario would move the bottom tail of the parental schooling distribution well above the current mean in almost all cases yet still lead to very small changes in inequality for their children's human capital. Furthermore, despite finding strong associations between child cognitive scores and parental human capital and per capita consumption for all countries, these scenarios with substantial changes for the parents in the bottom tail of the distribution do very little to decrease poverty (in the sense of the proportion of children below the 20th percentile of the distribution before the simulated change) or inequality for their children. The authors conclude that while increases in parental schooling attainment and per capita consumption for poor households are likely to be desirable in themselves to improve welfare, they are not likely to have large impacts on reducing human capital (and eventually probably adult per-capita consumption), poverty, and certainly not inequality in the next generation of adults. Thus, investing in programs to increase parental schooling and income is without a doubt a worthy objective, but doing so with the expectation that important benefits include that this would bring down substantially the prevalence of poverty and inequality in the next generation would be misguided. This study, thus, suggests that higher schooling and income for poor parents has limited effect on intergenerational mobility.

Simulations of Impacts of Human-Capital Investments Targeted Toward the Low End of the Earnings Distribution in Chile

Human-resource investments targeted toward the lower part of wage rate, earnings, or income distributions are often thought to be major means through which the persistent high LMIC inequalities in general, including those in Chile, might effectively be addressed, with concomitant effects of reducing poverty. Will such human resource interventions, if well targeted, reduce substantially inequality and poverty? To partially explore this question, in this study (Behrman, 2009) the Chilean 2004 Social Protection Survey (SPS) data are used to examine the impact of schooling attainment, using wage rate and earnings functions that probably are optimistic about the impact of schooling (because they ignore such factors as ability bias and market-level effects). Alternative simulations suggest significant impacts of well-targeted increases in schooling attainment on reducing inequality and poverty headcounts in schooling, earnings, and wage rates. They also illustrate the desirability of targeting directly toward the outcome of interest (e.g., toward those with low wage rates, not low schooling, if full income is of primary concern) despite the possible difficulties in doing so (since wage experiences typically are not revealed until after most people have completed schooling). But, though the magnitudes of some of the simulated impacts on the poverty headcounts are fairly large, the magnitudes of the reductions in the Gini coefficient estimates for earnings and for wage rates are not very large even though the simulated changes in schooling attainment are considerable. All in all these simulations suggest that while there is significant scope for reducing inequality and probably somewhat more poverty through human-capital interventions, expectations should not be for massive changes through these mechanisms alone unless there really are massive improvements in the human capital of the poorer members of society.

Roles of Macro and Educational Policy Contexts in Moderating Effects of Parental Family Background on Children's Schooling in Latin America

This study of a large number of Latin American and Caribbean countries over many years finds that family backgrounds have significant associations with children's schooling (Behrman et al., 2000). Children of higher-income and more-schooled parents everywhere and at all times are likely to do better, but there is substantial variation across countries and periods, depending on macroeconomic conditions and on public educational policy. Macro conditions – in particular those related to the extent of internal market development – importantly shape intergenerational mobility by loosening the strong link between parents' background and children's schooling. Similarly, educational policies can loosen that link, thus enhancing mobility. Increasing public resources available for basic schooling in general and for improving school quality in particular has a important positive impact on intergenerational schooling mobility. Raising other educational expenditures, however, such as those on tertiary education, may reinforce the impacts of family backgrounds and reduce intergenerational mobility. The study concludes that even though the immediate effects of macro-market reforms and schooling-policy reforms on current income distribution may not have been that strong, there may be important longer-run effects through increasing intergenerational social mobility. Another study for Brazil reports that the returns to schooling in standard earnings relations depend importantly on the macro conditions at the time of school completion, presumably because in boom times graduates are employed sooner and in better jobs with persistent effects over their working lives (Behrman and Birdsall, 1988).

6 Conclusions

Overall Summary

Parental investments in their children may play significant roles in affecting children's human capital and therefore distribution and poverty in the children's generation and absolute and relative intergenerational and intragenerational mobility. Children's human capital is of considerable interest in itself because of the positive impacts on children's productivities and welfare, as well as because of their relevance for overall development and social mobility. But it is important, particularly for LMICs, to include a wider definition of human capital than just, for example, schooling attainment on which much of the literature has focused. In particular in many LMICs physical health and nutritional status are important dimensions of children's human capital, especially for the early lifecycle stages. As such they may be channels through which parental human capital and endowments affect how children develop over their lifecycles and thus their welfare, productivities, the distribution of incomes and other outcomes, and social mobility. Also estimates of how observed components of human capital and endowments affect children's human capital and various outcomes in a number of cases vary considerably from simple associations – in some cases are considerably larger with control for measurement error and nonlinearities and in a number of cases are much smaller with control for unobserved endowments for which human capital in part may be serving as proxies in simple regressions. Moreover, the unobserved parental endowments related, for example, to genetic endowments, family culture, and family connections, often have substantial effects on the limited number of studies that explore these endowments with the implication that focusing only on the observed components is likely to be misleading and overstate the influence of observed parental characteristics such as schooling attainment and the extent of social mobility since these endowments are not likely to be affected by policy interventions even if observed parental and child human capital may be affected by policies.

As with any empirical topic, moreover, it is unlikely that any single characterization of parental human capital and endowments and children's human capital and social mobility fits all or most LMICs. There is too much heterogeneity in contexts – market development, policies, culture, demography, resources. Parental knowledge about various dimensions of and inputs into child development, for example, may be useful only if there are considerable market or policy alternatives. The incentives to invest in various dimensions of child development also are likely to depend importantly on current and expected future macro developments.

The estimates summarized in the previous sections suggest that parental human capital and endowments often have significant effects directly or indirectly on children's human capital and related outcomes and thus potentially distribution in the children's generation and intergenerational and intragenerational mobility. These effects tend to be larger in a number of studies for those who are thought to be more vulnerable, such as those who are undernourished, girls, or from low-SES families. But in many, though not all, cases the effects are much smaller than would be suggested by the simple associations presented in much of the literature once there is control for unobserved endowments. By itself, this may suggest that parental influence on children's human capital and therefore social persistence is less and social mobility greater that might seem to be the case from simple intergenerational and intragenerational associations of observed variables. However this may be misleading regarding the extent of parental influence on children's human capital and on social mobility because the serially correlated unobserved endowments both across and within generations increase persistence and limit social mobility.

Gaps in the Literature

There are many gaps in the literature on parental investments in their children, distributional effects, and social mobility in LMICs. Most of these gaps arise from data limitations. One sense in which data are limited is with regard to the critical components of human capital, characterized in this book as cognitive skills, socioemotional skills and health and nutritional status. The data are most limited with respect to mental health and socioemotional skills and parenting style as in Glewwe et al. (2017), for which reason there has been no or little exploration of these factors as part of the parental determinants of children's human capital or as dimensions of children's human capital that are affected by parental investments in LMICs, with the result that interesting conjectures posed about mental health and socioemotional skills in HICs are mostly unexplored for LMICs. But the data are also limited with respect to cognitive skills, with quite limited availability for parents and broader, but still fairly limited availability for their children. There also are limitations with regard to indicators of physical health, with much focus on child anthropometric indicators but more limited indicators over other parts of the lifecycle.

Another major data limitation is with respect to having longitudinal data that permit controlling for biases due to measurement errors, endogeneity, and unobserved factors. Experimental data are potentially powerful for these purposes, but there are very few data sets with relevant experiments long enough ago to control for parental human capital and endowments that also have data over substantial segments of their children's lifecycles, particularly into young and mature adulthood. So in most cases the only options are quasi-experimental methods, but the data needed for such methods are also relatively rare. For example there are relatively few data sets in LMICs on adult siblings in general and on adult twins in particular – I am only aware of one for the latter (for Chinese urban areas, studies with which are discussed above). And other plausible instruments for parental human capital and endowments in longitudinal data with sufficient information on the children also are rare, though successful efforts to link historical administrative data to micro intergenerational data have increased recently. Another possibility that has been used increasingly in HICs is genetic data, but I am not aware of any such use yet for the topics covered in this book for LMICs (Fletcher and Lehrer, 2011; Cook and Fletcher, 2014; Cook and Fletcher, 2015; Amin et al., 2017; Amin et al., 2021).

Another data limitation is that most longitudinal data with information on two generations have not yet followed the children long enough or have information on the parents when they were young enough to permit intergenerational comparisons at the comparable points in the lifecycle, so estimates of intergenerational social mobility confound lifecycle changes with intergenerational changes. And there is evidence that it is important to make intergenerational comparisons at comparable points in the lifecycle given the considerable changes that occur over the lifecycle, including during young adulthood what typically is characterized by many transitions including in the labor market and the early aging in many LMICs compared to HICs.

Yet another significant data limitation is that there are only a few studies for LMICs on what determines parental beliefs related to reference points, the underlying production technologies and expected returns for child investments, what impacts those beliefs have, and what determines those beliefs. Since the few studies that are reviewed above on relevant beliefs in LMICs suggest that actual beliefs may differ significantly from those on which parents make investment decisions in their children, more investigation of what determines such parental beliefs and how they affect investments in children's human capital would be useful. If parental beliefs about expected labor market returns to their children's human capital, for example, depend on recent macro experience in the economies in which they live, then one of the number of different ways in which contexts may matter is with regard to expectations for such returns.

Likewise, there are relatively few studies that directly address the constraints that capital markets place on investments in children, with most of the relevant studies making indirect inferences based on significant associations of such investments with parental resources, particularly for poorer households. Collection and use of more direct information on capital market access may be very informative for developing better policies.

In addition to these data limitations there also are important methodological limitations with regard to controlling for context in order to be more confident about external validity across space and time (Heckman and Feng, 2018). Indeed many studies are interpreted to have generalizable results without any serious effort for dealing with varying contexts. There are several exceptions, but they are notable as exceptions to the general practice of ignoring the probable importance of contexts. These exceptions include studies that use comparable data from very different contexts and test for differences in the estimated relations – an example is some of the studies using the Young Lives data from Ethiopia, India, Peru, and Vietnam. Another exception is studies that use other data to control for context, such as the macro data in the last study summarized in the previous section. A third exception is studies that use structural models (e.g., Todd and Wolpin, 2006; Attanasio et al., 2012) that, at least in principle, could be used to show how results are sensitive to different market and other contexts.

Another limitation of the available studies on social mobility in LMICS is that the LMIC intergenerational studies tend to focus on parents and children, though there are a few studies that do consider the roles of grandparents at least in predicting child outcomes (Zeng and Xie, 2014; Reynolds et al., 2018) and other studies that use twins and other siblings fixed effects to control, inter alia, for all past generations and other kin and ethnic group membership in their estimates of intergenerational effects of observed parental human capital and endowments (Li et al., 2010; Li et al., 2012; Rosenzweig and Zhang, 2013; Behrman et al., 2015; Hu et al., 2021). In contrast studies on HICs have moved increasingly toward investigating multiple generations, in particular grandparents, and tend to conclude that the significance of associations with grandparents implies less intergenerational social mobility than do two-generational studies (though these interpretations are questionable due to the failure to deal with intergenerationally correlated endowments as discussed at the end of Section 2) (Mare, 2011; Pfeffer, 2014; Solon, 2014; Park et al., 2022). Given that extended families, other kin support, and ethnic group support for human capital investments in children appear to be much more common in LMICs than in HICs, extending the LMIC literature on social mobility to multiple generations and other kin and ethnic group members seems to be a promising direction to pursue and is likely to reduce estimates of social mobility in LMICs. One of the relatively few LMIC studies to date, for low-income communities in India, suggests that new networks providing mutual support to their members and substituting for inherited parental human capital and wealth strengthen most rapidly in historically disadvantaged communities, generating a correspondingly high level of intergenerational mobility (Munshi, 2011). Such studies, of course, need to address the concerns about measurement errors and intergenerationally correlated unobserved endowments that are discussed at the end of Section 2.

Still another limitation of many studies of relations between parental investment in their children's human capital and inequalities in the children's generation and intergenerational mobility in LMICs (and HICs as well (Mogstad, 2017)) is that they tend to focus on one outcome, such as schooling attainment, which may reflect only a part of the intergenerational interaction. If some parents not only invest in their children's schooling attainment, but also in the quality of their schooling and transfer other resources, the patterns of intergenerational correlations in schooling probably are a misleading representation of the extent of parental impact on children's human capital, distribution, and mobility. For example, intergenerational land transfers are important for many people in many LMICs and if they are not taken into account in examining intergenerational schooling mobility the total intergenerational mobility may be misunderstood (probably overestimated) including gender dimensions (Quisumbing, 1994; Quisumbing and Otsuka, 2001; Bevis and Barrett, 2015). For another example, social capital may be intergenerationally transferred and enhance the returns to human capital (Rungo and Pena-Lopez, 2019). For yet another example, school quality, not only schooling attainment, may be important and, indeed, in one study in Brazil of standard earnings functions school quality crudely measured by teachers' schooling attainment is consistent with about as much of the variation in wages as is schooling attainment (Behrman and Birdsall, 1983).

Yet another limitation of most existing studies on parental investments in their children's human capital in LMICs is the dominance of partial-equilibrium approaches. For the questions of interest, which typically concern investments in the human capital of many children not just one child, approaches that include market-wide and general-equilibrium considerations such as the impact on expected returns to education if there were a large expansion in education would seem to add new insight on question such as would the supply expansion dominate to cause declines in the rates of return to education or might there be partially offsetting demand expansions?

Another way in which the literature on parental investments in their children and effects on distribution and social mobility in LMICs usefully could be extended is to integrate better the estimates on possible mechanisms with direct estimates of distributional effects or social mobility per se. Some possible mechanisms are reviewed in Sections 3 and 4. But there are others. For example, early life nutrition is found to affect ages of menarche and ages of first childbirth in India and ages of partnering, quality of partners, and ages of first births in Guatemala – all of which may affect individual and household adult income and well-being, as well as social mobility (Hoddinott et al., 2013b; Nandi et al., 2020). Better integration of mechanisms probably would be useful in illuminating better policy channels that might be promising for changing investments in children's human capital and their associated productivities, welfare, distribution, and social mobility.

A further way in which the literature on parental investments in their children and effects on distribution and social mobility in LMICs usefully could be extended would be to delve further into the underlying mechanisms, contexts, and estimation strategies that lead to some of the heterogeneities noted above in, for example, credit market effects and gender differences. Better understanding of such differences would be valuable in understanding to what extent such differences are real or are the results of differing methodologies.

The studies reviewed in this book, finally, primarily address parental investments in the human capital of their children and, relatedly, their productivities and welfare and effects on distribution in the children's generation and on absolute intergenerational mobility. More attention might usefully be directed toward how parental investments in the human capital of their children affect changes as the children pass through various lifecycle stages and thereby intragenerational mobility.

Thus, in recent years we have learned a lot about casual effects of parental investments on their children's human capital and, through that, human capital on levels and distributions of outcomes such as earnings and income and social mobility. This learning reflects a combination of increasingly rich data, mostly longitudinal, and improved approaches for undertaking such estimates. But, especially in light of the tremendous heterogeneities among LMIC contexts, the proverbial glass is much less than "half full." There remains many important unanswered questions on these topics and need for richer data and further explorations.

References

Abufhele-Milad, A. 2017. *Three Essays on Early Childhood Development from Chile*. Ph.D., University of Pennsylvania.

Abufhele, A., Behrman, J. & Bravo, D. 2017. Parental Preferences and Allocations of Investments in Children's Learning and Health within Families. *Social Science & Medicine*, 194, 76–86.

Acosta, P. A., Muller, N. & Sarzosa, M. 2015. *Beyond Qualifications: Returns to Cognitive and Socio-Emotional Skills in Colombia*. Bonn: Institute for the Study of Labor (IZA).

Adhvaryu, A., Molina, T., Nyshadham A. & Tamayo, J. Forthcoming. Helping Children Catch Up: Early Life Shocks and the PROGRESA Experiment. *Economic Journal*.

Alderman, H., Behrman, J., Lavy, V. & Menon, R. 2001a. Child Health and School Enrollment: A Longitudinal Analysis. *Journal of Human Resources*, 36, 185–205.

Alderman, H. & Behrman, J. R. 2006. Reducing the Incidence of Low Birth Weight In Low-Income Countries has Substantial Economic Benefits. *World Bank Research Observer*, 21, 25–48.

Alderman, H., Chiappori, P., Haddad, L., Hoddinott, J. & Kanbur, R. 1995. Unitary Versus Collective Models of the Household: Time to Shift the Burden of Proof? *World Bank Research Observer*, 10, 1–19.

Alderman, H. & Headey, D. D. 2017. How Important is Parental Education for Child Nutrition? *World Development*, 94, 448–464.

Alderman, H., Hoddinott, J. & Kinsey, B. 2001b. Long Term Consequences of Early Childhood Malnutrition. *The World Bank, Dalhousie University, University of Zimbabwe and Free University, Amsterdam, Mimeo*, 1–29.

Almond, D., Mazumder, B. & Van Ewijk, R. 2015. In Utero Ramadan Exposure and Children's Academic Performance. *The Economic Journal*, 125, 1501–1533.

Amin, V., Behrman, J. R., Fletcher, J. M. et al. 2021. Genetic Risks, Adolescent Health and Schooling Attainment. *Health Economics*, 30, 2905–2920.

Amin, V., Böckerman, P., Viinikainen, J. et al. 2017. Gene-Environment Interactions between Education and Body Mass: Evidence from the UK and Finland. *Social Science & Medicine*, 195, 12–16.

Andersen, C. T., Reynolds, S., Behrman, J. R. et al. 2015. Participation in the Juntos Conditional Cash Transfer Program in Peru Is Associated with Changes in Child Anthropometric Status but Not Language Development or School Achievement. *Journal of Nutrition*, 145, 2396–2405.

Andrew, A., Attanasio, O., Augsburg, B. et al. 2020. Effects of a Home Visiting Intervention in the Slums of Cuttack, Odisha. *Journal of Child Psychology and Psychiatry*, 61(6), 644–52.

Ashenfelter, O. & Krueger, A. 1994. Estimates of the Economic Return to Schooling from a New Sample of Twins. *American Economic Review*, 84, 1157–74.

Attanasio, O., Cunha, F. & Jervis, P. 2019. Subjective Parental Beliefs. Their Measurement and Role Cambridge, MA: National Bureau of Economic Research Working Paper 26516.

Attanasio, O. P., Meghir, C. & Santiago, A. 2012. Education Choices in Mexico: Using a Structural Model and a Randomized Experiment to Evaluate PROGRESA. *The Review of Economic Studies*, 79, 37–66.

Avila, J. C., Downer, B., Arango, S. M. & Wong, R. 2018. The Moderating Role of Education in the Relationship Between Diabetes and Cognitive Function Among Mexican Older Adults. *Population Association of America Annual Meetings*.

Barham, T., Macours, K. & Maluccio, J. A. 2013. Boys' Cognitive Skill Formation and Physical Growth: Long-Term Experimental Evidence on Critical Ages for Early Childhood Interventions. *American Economic Review*, 103, 467–471.

Bassi, M., Busso, M., Urzúa, S. & Vargas, J. 2012. *Disconnected: Skills, Education and Employment in Latin America*, Washington, DC: Inter-American Development Bank.

Becker, G. S. (ed.) 1967. Ann Arbor: University of Michigan, Woytinsky Lecture.

Becker, G. S. 1991. *A Treatise on the Family*, Cambridge, MA: Harvard University Press.

Becker, G. S. & Tomes, N. 1976. Child Endowments and the Quantity and Quality of Children. *Journal of Political Economy*, 84, S143–S162.

Becker, G. S. & Tomes, N. 1986. Human Capital and the Rise and Fall of Families. *Journal of Labor Economics*, 4(3 Part I), S1–S39.

Behrman, J. R. 1988a. Intrahousehold Allocation of Nutrients in Rural India: Are Boys Favored? Do Parents Exhibit Inequality Aversion? *Oxford Economic Papers*, 40(1), 32–54.

Behrman, J. R. 1988b. Nutrition, Health, Birth Order and Seasonality: Intrahousehold Allocation in Rural India. *Journal of Development Economics*, 28(1), 43–63.

Behrman, J. R. 1997. *Women's Schooling and Child Education: A Survey*. Philadelphia: University of Pennsylvania.

Behrman, J. R. 2009. How Much Might Human Capital Policies Affect Earnings Inequalities and Poverty? *Estudios Economicos*, 36, 9–41.

Behrman, J. R. 2022. Social Mobility and Human Capital in Low- and Middle-Income Countries. In Vegard Iversen, A. K., and K. Sen (eds.) *Social Mobility in Developing Countries: Concepts, Methods, and Determinants*. Oxford: Oxford University Press

Behrman, J. R., Alderman, H. & Hoddinott, J. 2004. Hunger and Malnutrition. In Lomborg, B. (ed.) *Global Crises, Global Solutions*. Cambridge: Cambridge University Press.

Behrman, J. R. & Birdsall, N. M. 1983. The Quality of Schooling: Quantity Alone is Misleading. *American Economic Review*, 73, 928–946.

Behrman, J. R. & Birdsall, N. 1988. The Reward for Good Timing: Cohort Effects and Earnings Functions for Brazilian Males. *Review of Economics and Statistics*, 70(1), 129–135.

Behrman, J. R., Birdsall, N. M. & Székely, M. 2000. Intergenerational Mobility in Latin America: Deeper Markets and Better Schools Make a Difference. In Birdsall, N. M. & Graham, C. (eds.) *New Markets, New Opportunities? Economic and Social Mobility in a Changing World*. Washington, DC: Brookings Institution Press.

Behrman, J. R., Calderon, M. C., Preston, S. H. et al. 2009. Nutritional Supplementation of Girls Influences the Growth of their Children: Prospective Study in Guatemala. *American Journal of Clinical Nutrition*, 90, 1372–1379.

Behrman, J. R., Contreras, D., Palma, M. I. & Puentes, E. Forthcoming. Wealth Disparities for Early Childhood Anthropometrics and Skills: Evidence from Chilean Longitudinal Data. *Population Research and Policy Review*.

Behrman, J. R. & Deolalikar, A. B. 1990. The Intrahousehold Demand for Nutrients in Rural South India: Individual Estimates, Fixed Effects and Permanent Income. *Journal of Human Resources*, 25(4), 665–696.

Behrman, J. R., Fan, C. S., Wei, X. et al. 2022b. *Tutoring Efficacy, Household Substitution, and Student Achievement: Experimental Evidence from an After-School Tutoring Program in Rural China*. Hong Kong: The Chinese University of Hong Kong.

Behrman, J. R., Hoddinott, J. F., Maluccio, J. A. & Martorell, R. 2017a. Brains versus Brawn: Labor Market Returns to Intellectual and Physical Human Capital in a Poor Developing Country. *International Food Policy Research Institute Discussion Paper 1487*.

Behrman, J. R., Hoddinott, J. F., Maluccio, J. A. et al. 2014. What Determines Adult Cognitive Skills? Influences of Pre-School, School and Post-School Experiences in Guatemala. *Latin American Economic Review*, 23, 1–32.

Behrman, J. R. & Knowles, J. C. 1999. Household Income and Child Schooling in Vietnam. *World Bank Economic Review*, 13, 211–256.

Behrman, J. R., Parker, S. W. & Todd, P. E. 2011. Do Conditional Cash Transfers for Schooling Generate Lasting Benefits?: A Five-Year Followup of PROGRESA/Oportunidades. *Journal of Human Resources*, 46, 93–122.

Behrman, J. R., Parker, S. W. & Todd, P. E. 2013. Incentives for Students and Parents. In Glewwe, P. (ed.) *Education Policy in Developing Countries*. Chicago: University of Chicago.

Behrman, J. R., Parker, S. W., Todd, P. E. & Wolpin, K. I. 2015 Aligning Learning Incentives of Students and Teachers: Results from a Social Experiment in Mexican High Schools. *Journal of Political Economy*, 123, 325–364.

Behrman, J. R., Parker, S. W., Todd, P. E. & Zhang, W. 2021. *Prospering through Prospera: CCT Impacts on Educational Attainment and Achievement in Mexico*. Philadelphia, PA: University of Pennsylvania.

Behrman, J. R., Pollak, R. A. & Taubman, P. 1982a. Parental Preferences and Provision for Progeny. *Journal of Political Economy*, 90(1), 52–73.

Behrman, J. R., Pollak, R. A. & Taubman, P. 1982b. Parental Preferences and Provision for Progeny. *Journal of Political Economy*, 90(1), 52–73.

Behrman, J. R., Pollak, R. A. & Taubman, P. 1986. Do Parents Favor Boys? *International Economic Review*, 27(1), 31–52.

Behrman, J. R., Pollak, R. A. & Taubman, P. 1995. The Wealth Model: Efficiency in Education and Equity in the Family. In Behrman, J. R., Pollak, R. A. & Taubman, P. (eds.) *From Parent to Child: Intrahousehold Allocations and Intergenerational Relations in the United States*. Chicago, IL: University of Chicago Press.

Behrman, J. R. & Rosenzweig, M. R. 2002. Does Increasing Women's Schooling Raise the Schooling of the Next Generation? *American Economic Review*, 92, 323–334.

Behrman, J. R., Rosenzweig, M. R. & Taubman, P. 1994. Endowments and the Allocation of Schooling in the Family and in the Marriage Market: The Twins Experiment. *Journal of Political Economy*, 102(6), 1131–1174.

Behrman, J. R., Schott, W., Mani, S. et al. 2017b. Intergenerational Transmission of Poverty and Inequality: Parental Resources and Schooling Attainment and Children's Human Capital in Ethiopia, India, Peru, and Vietnam. *Economic Development and Cultural Change*, 65, 657–697.

Behrman, J. R., Sengupta, P. & Todd, P. 2005. Progressing through PROGRESA: An Impact Assessment of a School Subsidy Experiment in Rural Mexico. *Economic Development and Cultural Change*, 54, 237–275.

Behrman, J. R. & Taubman, P. 1985. Intergenerational Earnings Mobility in the United States: Some Estimates and a Test of Becker's Intergenerational Endowments Model. *Review of Economics and Statistics*, 67(1), 141–151.

Behrman, J. R. & Taubman, P. 1986. Birth Order, Schooling and Earnings. *Journal of Labor Economics*, 4(4), S121–S145.

Behrman, J. R., Xiong, Y. & Zhang, J. 2015. Cross-Sectional Schooling-Health Associations Misrepresented Causal Schooling Effects on Adult Health and Health-Related Behaviors: Evidence from the Chinese Adults Twins Survey. *Social Science & Medicine*, 127, 190–197.

Berlinski, S., Galiani, S. & Gertler, P. 2009. The Effect of Pre-Primary Education on Primary School Performance. *Journal of Public Economics*, 93, 219–234.

Bevis, L. E. M. & Barrett, C. B. 2015. Decomposing Intergenerational Income Elasticity: The Gender-Differentiated Contribution of Capital Transmission in Rural Philippines. *World Development*, 74, 233–252.

Bhalotra, S., Delavande, A., Gilabert, P. F. & Maselko, J. 2020. Maternal Investments in Children: The Role of Expected Effort and Returns. Bonn: IZA Institute of Labor Economics Discussion Paper No. 13056.

Black, M. M., Behrman, J. R., Daelmans, B. et al. 2021. Nurturing Care Promotes Human Capital and Mitigates Adversities from Preconception through Adolescence. *British Medical Journal – Global Health*, 6, e004436.

Black, M. M., Walker, S. P., Fernald, L. et al. 2017. Early Childhood Development Coming of Age: Science through the Life Course. *The Lancet*, 389, 77–90.

Black, R. E., Liu, L., Hartwig, F. P. et al. Forthcoming. Health and Development from Preconception to 20 Years of Age to Build Human Capital. *The Lancet*.

Black, S. E., Devereux, P. J. & Salvanes, K. G. 2005. Why the Apple Doesn't Fall Far: Understanding Intergenerational Transmission of Human Capital. *The American Economic Review*, 95, 437–449.

Boneva, T. & Rauh, C. 2018. Parental Beliefs about Returns to Educational Investments – The Later the Better? *Journal of the European Economic Association*, 16, 1669–1711.

Britto, P. R., Lye, S. J., Proulx, K. et al. 2017. Nurturing Care: Promoting Early Childhood Development. *The Lancet*, 389, 91–102.

Chakraborty, T., Schüller, S. & Zimmermann, K. F. 2019. Beyond the Average: Ethnic Capital Heterogeneity and Intergenerational Transmission of Education. *Journal of Economic Behavior & Organization*, 163, 551–569.

Cook, C. J. & Fletcher, J. M. 2014. Interactive Effects of in Utero Nutrition and Genetic Inheritance on Cognition: New Evidence Using Sibling Comparisons. *Economics & Human Biology*, 13, 144–154.

Cook, C. J. & Fletcher, J. M. 2015. Can Education Rescue Genetic Liability for Cognitive Decline? *Social Science & Medicine*, 127, 159–170.

Crookston, B. T., Schott, W. B., Cueto, S. et al. 2013. Postinfancy Growth, Schooling, and Cognitive Achievement: Young Lives. *American Journal of Clinical Nutrition*, 98, 1555–1563.

Cueto, S., León, J., Miranda, A. et al. 2016. Does Pre-School Improve Cognitive Abilities among Children with Early-Life Stunting? A Longitudinal Study for Peru. *International Journal of Educational Research*, 75, 102–114.

Cunha, F., Elo, I. & Culhane, J. 2013. Eliciting Maternal Expectations about the Technology of Cognitive Skill Formation. Cambridge, MA: National Bureau of Economic Research Working Paper 19144.

Cunha, F., Heckman, J. & Schennach, S. 2010. Estimating the Technology of Cognitive and Noncognitive Skill Formation. *Econometrica*, 78, 883–931.

Cunha, F. & Heckman, J. J. 2008. Formulating, Identifying and Estimating the Technology of Cognitive and Noncognitive Skill Formation. *The Journal of Human Resources*, 43, 738–782

Cunha, F., Heckman, J. J., Lochner, L. J. & Masterov, D. V. 2006. Interpreting the Evidence on Life Cycle Skill Formation. In Hanushek, E. & Welch, F. (eds.) *Handbook of the Economics of Education*. 1st ed. Amsterdam: North-Holland.

Das, M. 2007. Persistent Inequality: An Explanation Based on Limited Parental Altruism. *Journal of Development Economics*, 84, 251–270.

De Onis, M., Blössner, M. & Borghi, E. 2010. Global Prevalence and Trends of Overweight and Obesity among Preschool Children. *The American Journal of Clinical Nutrition*, 92, 1257–1264.

De Onis, M., Blössner, M. & Borghi, E. 2011. Prevalence and Trends of Stunting among Pre-School Children, 1990–2020. *Public Health Nutrition*, 1, 1–7.

Dearden, K. A., Brennan, A. T., Schott, W. et al. 2017. Does Household Access to Improved Water and Sanitation in Infancy and Childhood Predict Better Vocabulary Test Performance in Ethiopian, Indian, Peruvian, and Vietnamese Cohort Studies? *BMJ Open*, 7, e013201.

Deutscher, N. & Mazumder, B. 2021. Measuring Intergenerational Income Mobility: A Synthesis of Approaches. Federal Reserve Bank of Chicago, Working Paper, No. 2021–09.

Díaz, J. J., Arias, O. & Tudela, D. V. 2012. *Does Perseverance Pay as Much as Being Smart? The Returns to Cognitive and Non-Cognitive Skills in Urban Peru*. Washington, DC: World Bank.

Dizon-Ross, R. 2019. Parents' Beliefs About Their Children's Academic Ability: Implications for Educational Investments. *American Economic Review*, 109, 2728–65.

Doyle, O., Harmon, C. P., Heckman, J. J. & Tremblay, R. E. 2009. Investing in early Human Development: Timing and Economic Efficiency. *Economics & Human Biology*, 7, 1–6.

Duc, L. T. 2019. Household Wealth and Gender Gap Widening in Height: Evidence from Adolescents in Ethiopia, India, Peru, and Vietnam. *Economics & Human Biology*, 34, 208–215.

Duc, L. T. & Behrman, J. R. 2017. Heterogeneity in Predictive Power of Early Childhood Nutritional Indicators for Mid-Childhood Outcomes: Evidence from Vietnam. *Economics and Human Biology*, 26, 86–95.

Duflo, E. 2001. Schooling and Labor Market Consequences of School Construction in Indonesia: Evidence from an Unusual Policy Experiment. *The American Economic Review*, 91, 795–813.

Engle, P. L., Black, M. M., Behrman, J. R. et al. 2007. Strategies to Avoid the Loss of Developmental Potential in More Than 200 Million Children in the Developing World. *The Lancet*, 369, 229–242.

Engle, P. L., Fernald, L. C. H., Alderman, H. et al. 2011. Strategies for Reducing Inequalities and Improving Developmental Outcomes for Young Children in Low-Income and Middle-Income Countries. *Lancet*, 378, 1339–1353.

Fernald, L. C. H., Weber, A., Galasso, E. & Ratsifandrihamanana, L. 2011. Socioeconomic Gradients and Child Development in a Very Low Income Population: Evidence from Madagascar. *Developmental Science*, 14, 832–847.

Fiszbein, A. & Schady, N. 2009. Conditional Cash Transfers: Reducing Present and Future Poverty. Washington, DC: The World Bank.

Fletcher, J. M. & Lehrer, S. F. 2011. Genetic Lotteries within Families. *Journal of Health Economics*, 30, 647–659.

Georgiadis, A., Benny, L., Crookston, B. T. et al. 2016. Growth Trajectories from Conception through Middle Childhood and Cognitive Achievement at Age 8 Years: Evidence from Four Low- and Middle-Income Countries. *Social Science & Medicine: Population Health*, 2, 43–54.

Georgiadis, A., Benny, L., Dornan, P. & Behrman, J. 2021. Maternal Undernutrition in Adolescence and Child Human Capital Development Over the Life Course: Evidence from an International Cohort Study. *Economica*, 88, 942–68.

Gertler, P., Heckman, J., Pinto, R. et al. 2014. Labor Market Returns to an Early Childhood Stimulation Intervention in Jamaica. *Science*, 344, 998–1001.

Glewwe, P., Huang, Q. & Park, A. 2017. Cognitive Skills, Noncognitive Skills, and School-to-Work Transitions in Rural China. *Journal of Economic Behavior & Organization*, 134, 141–164.

Glewwe, P. & Jacoby, H. 1993. Delayed Primary School Enrollment and Childhood Malnutrition in Ghana. Washington, DC: World Bank, Living Standards Measurement Study Working Paper No. 98.

Glewwe, P. & Jacoby, H. 2004. Economic Growth and the Demand for Education: Is there a Wealth Effect? *Journal of Development Economics*, 74, 33–51.

Glewwe, P., Jacoby, H. G. & King, E. M. 2001. Early Childhood Nutrition and Academic Achievement: A Longtitudinal Analysis. *Journal of Public Economics*, 81, 315–368.

Grantham-Mcgregor, S., Adya, A., Attanasio, O. et al. 2020. Group Sessions or Home Visits for Early Childhood Development in India: A Cluster RCT. *Pediatrics*, 146, e2020002725.

Gunewardena, D., King, E. M. & Valerio, A. 2018. More Than Schooling: Understanding Gender Differences in the Labor Market When Measures of Skill Are Available. Washington, DC: World Bank Policy Research Working Paper 8588.

Haddad, L., Hoddinott, J. & Alderman, H. (eds.) 1996. *Intrahousehold Resource Allocation: Methods, Models, and Policy*, Baltimore, MD: The Johns Hopkins University Press for the International Food Policy Research Institute.

Headey, D. & Hoddinott, J. 2016. The Nutritional Impacts of Bangladesh's Green Revolution. *Agricultural Systems*, 149, 122–131.

Heckman, J. J. 2006. Skill Formation and the Economics of Investing in Disadvantaged Children. *Science*, 312, 1900–1902.

Heckman, J. J. & Feng, S. Z. 2018. China's Investments in Skills. *Frontiers of Economics in China*, 13, 531–558.

Heckman, J. J., Stixrud, J. & Urzua, S. 2006. The Effects of Cognitive and Noncognitive Abilities on Labor Market Outcomes and Social Behavior. *Journal of Labor Economics*, 24, 411–482.

Hirvonen, K., Hoddinott, J., Minten, B. & Stifel, D. 2017. Children's Diets, Nutrition Knowledge, and Access to Markets. *World Development*, 95, 303–315.

Hoddinott, J., Alderman, H., Behrman, J. R., Haddad, L. & Horton, S. 2013a. The Economic Rationale for Investing in Stunting Reduction. *Maternal and Child Nutrition*, 9(Suppl. 2), 69–82.

Hoddinott, J., Behrman, J. R., Maluccio, J. A. et al. 2013b. Adult Consequences of Growth Failure in Early Childhood. *The American Journal of Clinical Nutrition*, 98, 1170–1178.

Hoddinott, J., Maluccio, J. A., Behrman, J. R., Flores, R. & Martorell, R. 2008. Effect of a Nutrition Intervention During Early Childhood on Economic Productivity in Guatemalan Adults. *The Lancet*, 371, 411–416.

Hu, Y., Behrman, J. R. & Zhang, J. 2021. The Causal Effects of Parents' Schooling on Children's Schooling in Urban China. *Journal of Comparative Economics*, 49(1), 258–276.

Iversen, V., Krishna, A. & Sen, K. 2022. Introduction: The State of Knowledge about Social Mobility in the Developing World. In Iversen, V., Krishna, A. & Sen, K. (eds.) *Social Mobility in Developing Countries: Concepts, Methods, and Determinants, edited by Vegard Iversen, Anirudh Krishna, and Kunal Sen,*. Oxford: Oxford University Press.

Jacoby, H. 1994. Borrowing Constraints and Progress through School: Evidence from Peru. *The Review of Economics and Statistics*, 76, 151–160.

Jensen, R. 2010. The (Perceived) Returns to Education and the Demand for Schooling. *Quarterly Journal of Economics*, 125, 515–548.

Jones, P. 1998. Skill Formation and Inequality in Poor Countries: How much do Ethnic Neighbourhoods Matter? *Journal of African Economies*, 7, 62–90.

King, E. M. & Lillard, L. A. 1987. Education Policy and Schooling Attainment in Malaysia and the Philippines. *Economics of Education Review*, 6(2), 167–181.

Kobayashi, L., Berkman, L., Wagner, R. et al. 2018. Height, Education, and Cognitive Function in a Population-Based Study of Older Men and Women in Rural South Africa. Population Association of America Annual Meetings.

Kohler, I. V., Payne, C. F., Bandawe, C. & Kohler, H.-P. 2018. Longitudinal Changes in Cognitive Health Among Mature Adults in a Low-Income Sub-Saharan African Context. *Population Association of America Annual Meetings*.

Kowalski, A., Georgiadis, A., Behrman, J. R. et al. 2018. Linear Growth through 12 Years is Weakly but Consistently Associated with Language and Math Achievement Scores at Age 12 Years in Four Low- or Middle-Income Countries. *Journal of Nutrition*, 148, 1852–1859.

Li, H., Liu, P. W. & Zhang, J. 2012. Estimating Returns to Education Using Twins in Urban China. *Journal of Development Economics*, 97, 494–504.

Li, H., Rosenzweig, M. & Zhang, J. 2010. Altruism, Favoritism, and Guilt in the Allocation of Family Resources: Sophie's Choice in Mao's Mass Send-Down Movement. *Journal of Political Economy*, 118, 1–38.

Lillard, L. & Willis, R. 1994. Intergenerational Education Mobility: Effects of Family and State in Malaysia. *Journal of Human Resources*, 29(4), 1126–1166.

Lillard, L. A. & Kilburn, M. R. 1995. Intergenerational Earnings Links: Sons and Daughters. *Santa Monica, CA: The RAND Corporation, Mimeo*.

Lillard, L. A. & Willis, R. J. 1997. Motives for Intergenerational Transfers: Evidence from Malaysia. *Demography*, 34, 115–134.

Liu, X., Behrman, J., Hannum, E., Wang, F. & Zhao, Q. 2022. Same Environment, Stratified Impacts? Air Pollution, Extreme Temperatures, and Birth Weight in South China. *Social Science Research,* 102691.

Liu, X., Behrman, J. R., Stein, A. D. et al. 2017. Prenatal Care and Child Growth and Schooling in Four Low- and Medium-Income Countries. *PloS One*, 12, e0171299.

Lopez-Boo, F. 2013. *Intercontinental Evidence on Socioeconomic Status and Early Childhood Cognitive Skills: Is Latin America Different?* Washington, DC: Inter-American Development Bank.

Lu, C., Black, M. M. & Richter, L. M. 2016. Risk of Poor Development in Young Children in Low-Income and Middle-Income Countries: An Estimation and Analysis at the Global, Regional, and Country Level. *The Lancet Global Health*, 4, e916-e922.

Maccini, S. & Yang, D. 2009. Under the Weather: Health, Schooling, and Economic Consequences of Early-Life Rainfall. *American Economic Review*, 99, 1006–26.

Majid, M. F. 2015. The Persistent Effects of in Utero Nutrition Shocks Over the Life Cycle: Evidence From Ramadan Fasting. *Journal of Development Economics*, 117, 48–57.

Majid, M. F., Jere R. Behrman & Mani, S. 2019. Short- and Long-Term Distributional Consequences of Prenatal Malnutrition and Stress: Using Ramadan as a Natural Experiment. *British Medical Journal Global Health*, 4, e001185.

Maluccio, J. A. 1998. Endogeneity of Schooling in the Wage Function: Evidence from the Rural Philippines. Washington, DC: International Food Policy Research Institute, FCND Discussion Paper 54.

Maluccio, J. A., Hoddinott, J. F., Behrman, J. R. et al. 2009. The Impact of Nutrition During Early Childhood on Education among Guatemalan Adults. *Economic Journal*, 119, 734–763.

Manley, J., Gitter, S. & Slavchevska, V. 2013. How Effective are Cash Transfers at Improving Nutritional Status? *World Development*, 48, 133–155.

Mare, R. D. 2011. A Multigenerational View of Inequality. *Demography*, 48, 1–23.

Mazumder, B., Rosales-Rueda, M. & Triyana, M. 2019. Intergenerational Human Capital Spillovers: Indonesia's School Construction and Its Effects on the Next Generation. *AEA Papers and Proceedings, American Economic Association*, 109, 243–249.

Mckee, D. & Todd, P. E. 2011. The longer-Term Effects of Human Capital Enrichment Programs on Poverty and Inequality: Oportunidades in Mexico. *Estudios de Economía*, 38, 67–100.

Mogstad, M. 2017. The Human Capital Approach to Intergenerational Mobility. *Journal of Political Economy*, 125, 1862–1868.

Munshi, K. 2011. Strength in Numbers: Networks as a Solution to Occupational Traps. *Review of Economic Studies*, 78, 1069–1101.

Nandi, A., Ashok, A., Kinra, S., Behrman, J. R. & Laxminarayan, R. 2016. Early Childhood Nutrition Is Positively Associated with Adolescent Educational Outcomes: Evidence from the Andhra Pradesh Child and Parents Study (APCAPS). *Journal of Nutrition*, 146, 806–813.

Nandi, A., Behrman, J. R., Black, M. M., Kinra, S. & Laxminarayan, R. 2020. Relationship between Early-Life Nutrition and Ages at Menarche and First Pregnancy, and Childbirth Rates of Young Adults: Evidence from APCAPS in India. *Maternal & Child Nutrition*, 16, e12854.

Nandi, A., Shet, A., Behrman, J. R. et al. 2019. Anthropometric, Cognitive, and Schooling Benefits of Measles Vaccination: Longitudinal Cohort Analysis in Ethiopia, India, and Vietnam. *Vaccine*, 37, 4336–4343.

Nordman, C. J., Sarr, L. R. & Sharma, S. 2015. Cognitive, Non-Cognitive Skills and Gender Wage Gaps: Evidence from Linked Employer-Employee Data in Bangladesh. Bonn: IZA Discussion Paper No. 9132.

Park, H., Choi, J., Behrman, J. R., Elo, I. & Smith K. R. 2022. Heterogeneous Associations between Grandparents and Grandchildren by Lineage and Gender in Ages at First Marriage and First Birth. Philadelphia, PA: University of Pennsylvania.

Pfeffer, F. T. 2014. Multigenerational Approaches to Social Mobility. A Multifaceted Research Agenda. *Research in Social Stratification and Mobility*, 35, 1–12.

Pitt, M. M., Rosenzweig, M. R. & Gibbons, D. M. 1993. The Determinants and Consequences of the Placement of Government Programs in Indonesia. *The World Bank Economic Review*, 7(3), 319–348.

Pollak, R. A. 1985. A Transaction Cost Approach to Families and Households. *Journal of Economic Literature*, 23, 581–608.

Psacharopoulos, G. & Patrinos, H. A. 2004. Returns to Investment in Education: A Further Update. *Education Economics*, 12, 111–134.

Puentes, E., Wang, F., Behrman, J. R. et al. 2016. Early Life Height and Weight Production Functions with Endogenous Energy and Protein Inputs. *Economics & Human Biology*, 22, 65–81.

Quisumbing, A. R. 1994. Intergenerational Transfers in Philippine Rice Villages: Gender Differences in Traditional Inheritance Customs. *Journal of Development Economics*, 43(2), 167–196.

Quisumbing, A. R. & Otsuka, K. 2001. Land Inheritance and Schooling in Matrilineal Societies: Evidence from Sumatra. *World Development*, 29, 2093–2110.

Reynolds, S. A., Andersen, C., Behrman, J. et al. 2017a. Disparities in Children's Vocabulary and Height in Relation to Household Wealth and

Parental Schooling: A Longitudinal Study in Four Low- and Middle-Income Countries. *SSM – Population Health*, 3, 767–786.

Reynolds, S. A., Fernald, L. C. H. & Behrman, J. R. 2017b. Mothers' Labor Market Choices and Child Development Outcomes in Chile. *SSM – Population Health*, 3, 756–766.

Reynolds, S. A., Fernald, L. C. H., Deardorff, J. & Behrman, J. R. 2018. Family Structure and Child Development in Chile: A Longitudinal Analysis of Household Transitions Involving Fathers and Grandparents. *Demographic Research*, 38, 1777–1814.

Richter, L. M., Daelmans, B., Lombardi, J. et al. 2017. Investing in the Foundation of Sustainable Development: Pathways to Scale Up for Early Childhood Development. *The Lancet*, 389, 103–118.

Rose, E. 1999. Consumption Smoothing and Excess Female Mortality in Rural India. *The Review of Economics and Statistics*, 81, 41–49.

Rose, E. 2000. Gender Bias, Credit Constraints and Time Allocation in Rural India. *Economic Journal*, 110, 738–758.

Rosenzweig, M. R. & Schultz, T. P. 1982. Market Opportunities, Genetic Endowments, and Intrafamily Resource Distribution: Child Survival in Rural India. *American Economic Review*, 72(4), 803–815.

Rosenzweig, M. R. & Schultz, T. P. 1984. Market Opportunities and Intrafamily Resource Distribution: Reply. *American Economic Review*, 74(3), 521–523.

Rosenzweig, M. R. & Zhang, J. 2013. Economic Growth, Comparative Advantage, and Gender Differences in Schooling Outcomes: Evidence from the Birthweight Differences of Chinese Twins. *Journal of Development Economics*, 104, 245–260.

Rungo, P. & Pena-Lopez, A. 2019. Persistent Inequality and Social Relations: An Intergenerational Model. *Journal of Mathematical Sociology*, 43, 23–39.

Sánchez, A., Meléndez, G. & Behrman, J. R. 2020. Impact of Juntos Conditional Cash Transfer Program on Nutritional and Cognitive Outcomes in Peru: Comparison between Younger and Older Initial Exposure. *Economic Development and Cultural Change*, 68, 865–897.

Schady, N., Behrman, J., Araujo, M. C. et al. 2015. Wealth Gradients in Early Childhood Cognitive Development in Five Latin American Countries. *Journal of Human Resources*, 50, 446–463.

Schott, W., Aurino, E., Penny, M. E. & Behrman, J. R. 2019. The Double Burden of Malnutrition among Youth: Trajectories and Inequalities in Four Emerging Economies. *Economics & Human Biology*, 34, 80–91.

Schott, W., Crookston, B. T., Lundeen, E. A. et al. 2013. Child Growth from Ages 1 to 8 Years in Ethiopia, India, Peru and Vietnam: Key Distal Household and Community Factors. *Social Science & Medicine*, 97, 278–287.

Schultz, T. P. 1990. Testing the Neoclassical Model of Family Labor Supply and Fertility. *Journal of Human Resources*, 25(4), 599–634.

Schultz, T. P. 2004. School Subsidies for the Poor: Evaluating the Mexican Progresa Poverty Program. *Journal of Development Economics*, 74, 199–250.

Soler-Hampejsek, E., Mensch, B. S., Psaki, S. R. et al. 2018. Reading and Numeracy Skills after School Leaving in Southern Malawi: A Longitudinal Analysis. *International Journal of Educational Development*, 59, 86–99.

Solon, G. 2002. Cross-Country Differences in Intergenerational Earnings Mobility. *The Journal of Economic Perspectives*, 16, 59–66.

Solon, G. 2014. Theoretical Models of Inequality Transmission across Multiple Generations. *Research in Social Stratification and Mobility*, 35, 13–18.

Taubman, P. & Behrman, J. R. 1986. Effect of Number and Position of Siblings on Child and Adult Outcomes. *Social Biology*, 33, 22–34.

Thomas, D. 1990. Intrahousehold Resource Allocation: An Inferential Approach. *Journal of Human Resources*, 25(4), 635–664.

Thomas, D. 1993. The Distribution of Income and Expenditure within the Household. *Annales de Economie et de Statistiques*, 29, 109–136.

Thomas, D. & Strauss, J. 1992. Prices, Infrastructure, Household Characteristics and Child Height. *Journal of Development Economics*, 39 (2), 301–332.

Thomas, D., Strauss, J. & Henriques, M. H. 1991. How Does Mother's Education Affect Child Height? *Journal of Human Resources*, 26(2), 183–211.

Todd, P. E. & Wolpin, K. I. 2006. Using a Social Experiment to Validate a Dynamic Behavioral Model of Child Schooling and Fertility: Assessing the Impact of a School Subsidy Program in Mexico. *American Economics Review*, 96, 1384–1417.

Torche, F. 2018. Prenatal Exposure to an Acute Stressor and Children's Cognitive Outcomes. *Demography*, 55, 1611–1639.

Torche, F. & Echevarría, G. 2011. The Effect of Birthweight on Childhood Cognitive Development in a Middle-Income Country. *International Journal of Epidemiology*, 40, 1008–1018.

Torche, F. & Villarreal, A. 2014. Prenatal Exposure to Violence and Birth Weight in Mexico: Selectivity, Exposure, and Behavioral Responses. *American Sociological Review*, 79, 966–992.

Trude, A. C. B., Richter, L. M., Behrman, J. R. et al. 2021. Effects of Responsive Caregiving and Learning Opportunities during Pre-School Ages on the Association of Early Adversities and Adolescent Human Capital: An Analysis of Birth Cohorts in Two Middle-Income Countries. *Lancet Child and Adolescent Health*, 5, 37–46.

United Nations Development Program. 2014. *Millennium Development Goals and Beyond* [Online]. New York: United Nations. www.un.org/millennium goals/education [Accessedon August 10, 2021].

Victora, C. G., Adair, L., Fall, C. et al. 2008. Maternal and Child Undernutrition: Consequences for Adult Health and Human Capital. *The Lancet*, 371, 340–357.

Victora, C. G., De Onis, M., Hallal, P. C., Blössner, M. & Shrimpton, R. 2010. Worldwide Timing of Growth Faltering: Revisiting Implications for Interventions. *Pediatrics*, 125, e473–e480.

Walker, S., Chang, S. M., Wright, A., Osmond C. & Grantham-Mcgregor, S. 2015. Early Childhood Stunting is Associated with Lower Developmental Levels in the Subsequent Generation of Children. *Journal of Nutrition*, 145, 823–828.

Walker, S. P., Chang, S. M., Vera-Hernández, M. & Grantham-Mcgregor, S. 2011. Early Childhood Stimulation Benefits Adult Competence and Reduces Violent Behavior. *Pediatrics*, 127(5), 849–857.

Wang, F., Puentes, E., Behrman, J. & Cunha, F. Forthcoming. You are What Your Parents Expect: Height and Local Reference Points. *Journal of Econometrics*.

Yi, J., Heckman, J., Zhang, J. & Conti, G. 2015. Early Health Shocks, Intrahousehold Resource Allocation, and Child Human Capital. *Economic Journal*, 128, F347–F371.

Zeng, Z. & Xie, Y. 2014. The Effects of Grandparents on Children's Schooling: Evidence From Rural China. *Demography*, 51, 599–617.

Zhang, H., Behrman, J. R., Fan, C. S., Wei, X. & Zhang, J. 2014. Does Parental Absence Reduce Cognitive Achievements? Evidence from Rural China. *Journal of Development Economics*, 111, 181–195.

Acknowledgments

I thank UNU-WIDER and Vegard Iversen, Anirudh Krishna, and Kunal Sen for inviting me to participate in the UNU-WIDER project on *Social Mobility in Developing Countries: Concepts, Methods and Determinants*, Anirudh Krishna and Markus Jäntti for useful comments on preliminary material related to this Element, and two anonymous reviewers for helpful comments on the first version of this manuscript. I retain all responsibility for the contents, including any errors or misinterpretations.

Cambridge Elements $\equiv$

Development Economics

Kunal Sen

UNU-WIDER, and University of Manchester

Kunal Sen, UNU-WIDER Director, is Editor-in-Chief of the Cambridge Elements in Development Economics series. Professor Sen has over three decades of experience in academic and applied development economics research, and has carried out extensive work on international finance, the political economy of inclusive growth, the dynamics of poverty, social exclusion, female labour force participation, and the informal sector in developing economies. His research has focused on India, East Asia, and sub-Saharan Africa. In addition to his work as Professor of Development Economics at the University of Manchester, Kunal has been the Joint Research Director of the Effective States and Inclusive Development (ESID) Research Centre, and a Research Fellow at the Institute for Labor Economics (IZA). He has also served in advisory roles with national governments and bilateral and multilateral development agencies, including the UK's Department for International Development, Asian Development Bank, and the International Development Research Centre.

Thematic Editors

Tony Addison

University of Copenhagen, and UNU-WIDER

Tony Addison is a Professor of Economics in the University of Copenhagen's Development Economics Research Group. He is also a Non-Resident Senior Research Fellow at UNU-WIDER, Helsinki, where he was previously the Chief Economist-Deputy Director. In addition, he is Professor of Development Studies at the University of Manchester. His research interests focus on the extractive industries, energy transition, and macroeconomic policy for development.

Chris Barret

Johnson College of Business, Cornell University

Chris Barrett is an agricultural and development economist at Cornell University. He is the Stephen B. and Janice G. Ashley Professor of Applied Economics and Management; and International Professor of Agriculture at the Charles H. Dyson School of Applied Economics and Management. He is also an elected Fellow of the American Association for the Advancement of Science, the Agricultural and Applied Economics Association, and the African Association of Agricultural Economists.

Carlos Gradín

UNU-WIDER, and University of Vigo

Carlos Gradín is a UNU-WIDER Research Fellow, and a professor of applied economics at the University of Vigo (on leave). His main research interest is the study of inequalities, with special attention to those that exist between population groups (e.g., by race or sex). His publications have contributed to improving the empirical evidence in developing and developed countries, as well as globally, and to improving the available data and methods used.

Rachel M. Gisselquist
UNU-WIDER

Rachel M. Gisselquist is a Senior Research Fellow and member of the Senior Management Team of UNU-WIDER. She specializes in the comparative politics of developing countries, with particular attention to issues of inequality, ethnic and identity politics, foreign aid and state building, democracy and governance, and sub-Saharan African politics. Dr Gisselquist has edited a dozen collections in these areas, and her articles are published in a range of leading journals.

Shareen Joshi
Georgetown University

Shareen Joshi is an Associate Professor of International Development at Georgetown University's School of Foreign Service in the United States. Her research focuses on issues of inequality, human capital investment and grassroots collective action in South Asia. Her work has been published in the fields of development economics, population studies, environmental studies and gender studies.

Patricia Justino
Senior Research Fellow, UNU-WIDER, and IDS – UK

Patricia Justino is a Senior Research Fellow at UNU-WIDER and Professorial Fellow at the Institute of Development Studies (IDS) (on leave). Her research focuses on the relationship between political violence, governance and development outcomes. She has published widely in the fields of development economics and political economy and is the co-founder and co-director of the Households in Conflict Network (HiCN).

Marinella Leone
University of Pavia

Marinella Leone is an assistant professor at the Department of Economics and Management, University of Pavia, Italy. She is an applied development economist. Her more recent research focuses on the study of early child development parenting programmes, on education, and gender-based violence. In previous research she investigated the short-, long-term and intergenerational impact of conflicts on health, education and domestic violence. She has published in top journals in economics and development economics.

Jukka Pirttilä
University of Helsinki, and UNU-WIDER

Jukka Pirttilä is Professor of Public Economics at the University of Helsinki and VATT Institute for Economic Research. He is also a Non-Resident Senior Research Fellow at UNU-WIDER. His research focuses on tax policy, especially for developing countries. He is a co-principal investigator at the Finnish Centre of Excellence in Tax Systems Research.

Andy Sumner
King's College London, and UNU-WIDER

Andy Sumner is Professor of International Development at King's College London; a Non-Resident Senior Fellow at UNU-WIDER and a Fellow of the Academy of Social Sciences. He has published extensively in the areas of poverty, inequality, and economic development.

About the Series

Cambridge Elements in Development Economics is led by UNU-WIDER in partnership with Cambridge University Press. The series publishes authoritative studies on important topics in the field covering both micro and macro aspects of development economics.

United Nations University World Institute for Development Economics Research

United Nations University World Institute for Development Economics Research (UNU-WIDER) provides economic analysis and policy advice aiming to promote sustainable and equitable development for all. The institute began operations in 1985 in Helsinki, Finland, as the first research centre of the United Nations University. Today, it is one of the world's leading development economics think tanks, working closely with a vast network of academic researchers and policy makers, mostly based in the Global South.

UNITED NATIONS
UNIVERSITY
UNU-WIDER

Cambridge Elements ☰

Development Economics

Elements in the Series

The 1918–20 Influenza Pandemic: A Retrospective in the Time of COVID-19
Prema-chandra Athukorala and Chaturica Athukorala

Parental Investments and Children's Human Capital in Low-to-Middle-Income Countries
Jere R. Behrman

A full series listing is available at: www.cambridge.org/CEDE